P9-BJI-185

Pitkin County Library

120 North Mill Street
Aspen, Colorado 81611

Modern British Music

Modern British Music

The Second British Musical Renaissance—
From Elgar to P. Maxwell Davies

Otto Karolyi

Rutherford ● Madison ● Teaneck
Fairleigh Dickinson University Press
London and Toronto: Associated University Presses

Associated University Presses
440 Forsgate Drive
Cranbury, NJ 08512

Associated University Presses
25 Sicilian Avenue
London WC1A 2QH, England

Associated University Presses
P.O. Box 338, Port Credit
Mississauga, Ontario
Canada L5G 4L8

The paper used in this publication meets the requirements
of the American National Standard for Permanence of Paper
for Printed Library Materials Z39.48-1984.

Library of Congress Cataloging-in-Publication Data

Karolyi, Otto, 1934–
    Modern British music : the second British musical renaissance—
from Elgar to P. Maxwell Davies / Otto Karolyi.
        p. cm.
    Includes bibliographical references and index.
    ISBN 0-8386-3532-6 (alk. paper)
    1. Music—Great Britain—20th century—History and criticism.
I. Title.
ML285.5.K33   1994
780'.941'0904—dc20   92-55105
                                                      CIP

PRINTED IN THE UNITED STATES OF AMERICA

To Benedikte

Contents

Foreword

It is hoped that the reader will find this book useful as a guide to the music included in its content and that it will serve to generate an enthusiasm for British music that will eventually lead beyond the introductory scope of this volume.

I should like here to express my thanks to my wife, Benedikte Uttenthal, for her loving support in reading the manuscript and good advice in matters of idiomatic English, to Juliet Middleton, Elspeth Gillespie, and Susan Sinclair for their generous help and patient typing and retyping of the manuscript, to Bill Macdonald for his encouraging and perceptive comments, to Richard E. Jones, Michael Koy, Paul Rieder, and Regina Phair of Associated University Presses, and finally thanks to my son, Julian, who volunteered to be one of the first critical "general readers."

Modern British Music

1

Romanticism and Postromanticism: Edward Elgar, Frederick Delius, Arnold Bax, John Ireland

I know that Elgar is not manic enough to be Russian, not witty or pointilliste enough to be French, not harmonically simple enough to be Italian and not stodgy enough to be German. We arrive at his Englishry by pure elimination.
—Anthony Burgess

Since the turn of the century, one of the most striking artistic developments in this country has manifested itself in music. Indeed, there has been a virtual revival of an art form that, for complex and not easily verifiable reasons, had been dormant since the end of the seventeenth century. Anyone surveying the past can have no doubt about the musical ability of Great Britain, a country that has contributed to European musical culture from the Middle Ages to Purcell's time—with varying importance at times, but certainly with continuity. Whether the impact of the Civil War—or the industrial revolution, with its scarring effect in brutally uprooting long-standing agricultural values in favor of quick gains in newly created factories and industrial towns—contributed to the more or less complete silencing of the indigenous musical muse is, of course, a matter of debate. So, too, is the suggestion of a native inclination towards pragmatism and a suspicion of the arts and artists in general. Be that as it may, the fact is that for two hundred years, during which time music was flourishing in the rest of western Europe, England contributed no composer of real substance. As Wilfrid Mellers has pointed out, it is, perhaps, not by chance that even in art forms based on language or vision, the least poetic genre, the novel gained the greatest popularity in nineteenth-century England. Music, the most poetic and abstract of all art forms, was denied its role as a serious and legitimate vehicle for thought and ideas. Generally speaking, from the end of the Renaissance, music slowly fell behind the other arts and became the Cinderella in the hierarchy of human expression; nowhere was this more markedly so than in England. When music is seen to be no more than entertainment and is reduced to being a diversion of no consequence, then native music is bound to stay dormant and subservient and to find an outlet in trivia such as the operetta. Entertaining as the Gilbert and Sullivan operettas are, they are nevertheless sadly symptomatic in representing the state of music in England in the nineteenth century. It seems that, in time, the English themselves began to believe in their own inferiority in matters musical, and the vogue for importing artists took the place of practising an art form that commanded but little respect and significance. In this context it is well worth remembering that Bax's father believed that his son's musical interest was an illness, and that when the young Britten boldly expressed his desire to be a composer, the reaction was "Yes, but what else?" No wonder that from Handel to the late nineteenth century the English musical scene was dominated by foreigners and by Austro-German models. It seems that material prosperity based on industrial misery is not necessarily conducive to musical culture.

Thus the nineteenth century became a musical desert in the history of the cultural and spiritual life of Great Britain. It was for this reason that the Germans made the notorious observation that England was a "land without music." That is not to say that music did not have a place in British life: there were several gifted musicians around, such as John Field, Hubert Parry, Charles Villiers Stanford, and Ethel Smyth, but none of these displayed real genius. It takes, however, but one genius to fill the vacuum, and England has been able to offer more than one since Elgar's time.

In Elgar one is confronted with a particularly characteristic English tendency in music, that of following at the tail end of European developments. Although he died in 1934, Elgar had nothing to do with modernism as such. His music is largely nostalgic and retrospective. He belongs to the "Last Mohicans" of romantic musical expression, not unlike Sergei Rachmaninov and Jean Sibelius, neither of whom had much sympathy with twentieth-century musical developments. These composers created their best musical output stylistically oblivious to, or perhaps in spite of, the fact that their world was gone forever. This is not to suggest that Sibelius's music is not great music. It is, but it is not modern. So, too, with Elgar who stands at the very threshold of the Second English Renaissance. It was his musical genius that broke the silence, or what is even worse, the musical mediocrity, which had befallen England for about two hundred years. Single-handedly he made up for the desert of the nineteenth-century romantic period in England and helped to create respect for native music-making. It is therefore appropriate that this brief survey of twentieth-century British music should begin with his name.

Sir Edward Elgar (1857–1934)

Elgar was born on 2 June 1857 at Broadheath near Worcester of art-loving and understanding parents. His father was a competent organist, pianist, and violinist who, in 1863, opened a music shop in Worcester. Edward, the fourth of seven children, spent his formative years living over the shop with his family. He showed his composing ability at the early age of about ten. Apart from violin lessons from a Worcester teacher, however, he never received any formal training in music. He was an entirely self-taught, self-made man who, from the age of sixteen, lived as a full-time but free-lance musician, turning his hand to every form of music-making from helping his father, to violin and organ playing, to conducting and taking part in the Three Choirs Festival* and becoming the bandmaster and composer for the lunatic asylum at Pounds. At the age of thirty-two he married a general's daughter, who was eight years his senior. This move up into a higher social class was an unusual event in those days, and it raised many eyebrows. The class consciousness that divides Britain to a bewildering extent even today was perhaps at its peak during El-gar's time, and it was a pressure Elgar himself never managed to overcome. He once declined an invitation to a party by sending a

---

*So called because of the meetings by rotation of three choirs from the cathedrals of Gloucester, Hereford, and Worcester.

note saying, "You would not wish your board to be disgraced by the presence of a piano tuner's son and his wife."

Elgar's mental makeup seems to encompass the grandiose and the pompous, a "chip on the shoulder" introversion together with the most noble qualities. In his wife Alice, however, he found all the encouragement and motherly support he needed. Indeed, such was his dependence on her that, after her death in 1920, he virtually gave up composing altogether.

His first real breakthrough came with the first performance of *Variations on an Original Theme (Enigma)*, op. 36 (1898–99). This is an extraordinary piece of music, one of the great set of orchestral variations of all time, in which each variation is a musical sketch of a friend, indicated by initials and pseudonyms. It is an orchestral piece with an aura: in some mysterious way it not only conveys the essential Elgar, but an Englishness also—and this in spite of the fact that the musical language is Austro-German and deeply indebted to Brahms, Schumann, and Richard Strauss. In fact, the *Enigma Variations* is his answer to Brahms's *Variations on a Theme by Haydn*, which was at the height of its popularity when Elgar wrote this essay in the same genre. The real enigma of the composition lies not so much in a hidden melody or message, but in the genius that forged out of a largely foreign idiom a truly English orchestral masterpiece.

His next major work was the result of a commission for a large-scale choral work for the 1900 Birmingham Festival. For this Elgar wrote an oratorio on the text of Cardinal Newman's poem *The Dream of Gerontius*, op. 38 (1899–1900). In this controversial work—of which Stanford said that "it stinks of incense," and later, in a more honest and less jealous moment, "I would have given my head to have written Part I of Gerontius"—Elgar gives expression to his Catholic faith in the form of a strange blend of the Handelian oratorio tradition with aspects of Wagner's musical thinking. Its first performance in Birmingham was a failure, which depressed Elgar for a while. Yet it was *The Dream of Gerontius* that brought him continental recognition by its second performance in Düsseldorf, after which Richard Strauss declared Elgar the foremost English composer. The oratorios written after *Gerontius*, *The Apostles*, op. 49 (1903), and *The Kingdom*, op. 50 (1901–6), are, in spite of the many fine moments in them, justifiably overshadowed by the great *Gerontius*.

The period between 1901 and 1914 marked Elgar's triumph. He was knighted in 1904; he wrote the *Cockaigne Overture,* op. 40 (1901), two symphonies: no. 1 in A flat major, op. 55 (1907–8) and no. 2 in E flat major, op. 63 (1903–11), the Violin Concerto, op. 61 (1909–10) (dedicated to Fritz Kreisler, the great Austrian violinist), the ode *The Music Makers,* op. 69 (1902–12) in which, most significantly, Elgar quotes the Enigma theme and the Nimrod variation, the *Introduction and Allegro for Strings,* op. 47 (1905), the symphonic study *Falstaff,* op, 68 (1902–13), and, of course, the majority of the *Pomp and Circumstance Marches,* op. 39 (1901–30). These brilliant and yet painfully imperialistic, jingoistic marches represent Elgar's Edwardian nationalism.

During the First World War, Elgar wrote some patriotic compositions of modest interest, such as the *Carillon,* op. 75 (1914), a recitation with orchestra in honor of Belgium, and *The Spirit of England,* op. 80 (1915–17), to texts by Binyon. His final creative phase lasted up until the death of his wife in 1920. During 1918 and 1919 he created a series of three distinguished chamber works: the Violin Sonata, op. 82, the String Quartet, op. 83, and the Piano Quintet, op. 84. But the penultimate achievement of Elgar's last creative period is his Cello Concerto, op. 85. The fact that this concerto was composed during 1918 and 1919 is telling. For Elgar, and for many others, it was the end of an era both in England and on the Continent. The romanticism of the late Victorian and Edwardian periods, so dear to Elgar, was over.

Apart from the *Pomp and Circumstance Marches* and the *Enigma Variations,* the Cello Concerto is perhaps Elgar's most popular composition. His ability to combine depth and lyricism with a popular style has made this concerto a cherished work in the repertoire. In spite of its four clearly defined movements, it is somewhat rhapsodic in character, and the opening cello theme serves as a unifying motto. It appears, for example, as a link to the scherzolike second movement and, most dramatically, as the conclusion of the fourth movement. The main theme of the first movement is pastoral in mood, a mood much liked by Elgar and one that subsequently became one of the stylistic hallmarks of British composers between the two world wars, with its quality of inducing patriotic nostalgia. The third movement is a passionate lament in which Elgar allows a glimpse of the inner sanctuary of his soul. The predominance of slow tempi and indications of recitative throughout the entire score reveal the contemplative and personal character of this work. The last movement, in spite of its Falstaffian quality, could have given way to melancholy, but this is abruptly cut off. An English understatement, or the musical equivalent of a stiff upper lip, closes this masterpiece. As so often in his compositions, Elgar gave the direction *nobilmente*—a key word towards an understanding of his music.

Frederick Delius (1862–1934)

Although Delius was a contemporary of Elgar, it would be hard to find a more different character both as a man and artist. A sensuous, epicurean personality of German origin, whose father was engaged in the wool trade in Bradford, he turned to music notwithstanding opposition from his family. His father's attempt to make his son a businessman in Florida, where the young Delius was sent to look after an orange plantation, failed spectacularly. Delius neglected the plantation and occupied himself instead with studying music. Yet he succeeded financially as a teacher of music in Danvill, Virginia, where the girls of a finishing school for Baptist young ladies had the pleasure of being taught by him. His father, impressed by the son's unexpected success (even though it was not the one he had hoped for), agreed to back his music studies at Leipzig. It was there that he encountered Edvard Grieg again, whom he had first met on a holiday in Norway in 1887 and who advised him to devote his life to music. Indeed, it was Grieg who later managed to persuade Delius's father that his son should stay on in Europe and go to Paris. There, among others, he met Maurice Ravel, Florent Schmitt, August Strindberg, Edvard Munch, and Paul Gauguin—from whom he purchased the painting *Nevermore*. It was there, too, that he met, in 1896, his wife-to-be, the painter Jelka Rosen.

Delius chose to settle in France, but his association with Norway and with Scandinavian culture gave him a constant source of inspiration. Many of his compositions are based on Scandinavian texts and demonstrate his familiarity with the writings of authors such as Henrik Ibsen and J. P. Jacobsen. In addition, some of his works show that his American experience had an influence: for example, the style of black music is displayed in *Appalachia, Variations of an Old Slave Song* (1896–1902). One of the most striking features of Delius's idiosyncratic style, however, is that, although he belongs to the post-Wagnerian world of Richard Strauss and Debussy, he remains a solitary figure in whose music a hyperromantic and hedonistic love of nature is given expression together with a worship of the instinctive. Moreover, in most of his music, external influences—that is, programmatic extra-musical elements—dominate. The monumental symphonic poem *Paris: The Song of a Great City* (1898–99), influenced by Richard Strauss, is Delius's nocturnal impression of the great city. It would, however, be a mistake to look for literal depiction in this music as it is, above all, an evocation of his moods. Chracteristically, it is much more an expression of Paris as experienced by Delius than an attempt to give a portrait of the city.

Delius was primarily preoccupied with an entirely subjective expression of the poetic in music. It is perhaps not by chance that he felt a natural affinity with the writings of Nietzsche. His large-scale choral work *A Mass of Life* (1904–8) is based on Nietzsche's *Also sprach Zarathustra*. It received its first complete performance in London (1909) under Beecham, who became Delius's most ardent advocate. In this work, as in most works of Delius, the non-Christian, pagan world, as romantically imagined by both himself and Nietzsche—in which the individual proudly strives for self-realisation—gains expression. Consequently, *A Mass of Life* is a vindication of life through the experience of the individual who faces up to his destiny. This is, therefore, not sacred music in the conventional Christian sense: Delius was particular in avoiding what he called the "Jesus element" in his compositions. Yet the ritualistic is there all the same. As Delius put it: "Music is a cry of the soul. It is a revelation, a thing to be reverenced. Performances of a great musical work are for us what rites and festivals of religion were to the ancients—an initiation into the mysteries of the human soul."[1]

The inherent danger of a hedonistic world view combined with an obsessive preoccupation with the self, however, is that it is founded on megalomania and can so easily slip into zones of sensuous sentimentality and onanistic nostalgia. At his worst, Delius, like his Russian contemporary Scriabin, can be monotonous and limited. On occasion the improvisationlike chromatic wanderings must have had more significance for the composer than they do for the listener. Yet at his best, as in *Sea Drift* (1903–4) for solo baritone, chorus, and orchestra (based on a text by Whitman, a poet with whom Delius had profound affinities) and in *A Song of the High Hills* (1911–12) for wordless chorus and orchestra (the same combination as Debussy used in his third Nocturne, *Sirenes*), Delius can lead the listener, as if by magic, to poetic experiences of great beauty.

This egotistic eccentric, who in his keenness for indpendence once stated, "I don't claim to be a British composer," was nevertheless also inspired to create a memorable work based on an English folk song from Lincolnshire, the opening lines of which are:

> It was on the fifth of August
> The weather fine and fair
> Unto Brigg Fair I did repair
> For love I was inclined.

Brigg Fair: An English Rhapsody (1907) is an orchestral variation on the folk theme that was introduced to Delius by the Australian composer Percy Grainger. In a characteristic way, Delius said: "I consider Percy Grainger the most gifted English composer and the only one who writes English music—and he is an Australian. . . ."[2]

Delius's last ten years, from 1924 to 1934, were made tragic by the syphilitic disease that rapidly paralysed and blinded him. As a helpless invalid he was looked after by his wife in their home at Grez. He defiantly carried on composing by dictating to his amanuensis Eric Fenby. One of these dictated works is a setting of poems by Whitman, for double chorus and orchestra, the *Songs of Farewell* (1920–22).

Sir Arnold Bax (1883–1953)

The music of Arnold Bax is nowadays seldom in evidence in the concert repertoire, yet, during the period of his popularity in the 1920s and 1930s (culminating in a knighthood in 1937), he seemed to be an equal even of Vaughan Williams, who has since eclipsed him. He was a brilliant pianist and prolific composer who had the ability to dazzle everyone. He came under the influences of Wagner, of Richard Strauss, and, more significantly, of Elgar. But the most striking formative impact on his work came about when this Englishman suddenly discovered the real or imaginary Celt in himself while reading W. B. Yeats's poetry. This encounter almost made him abandon music for the sake of literature. Indeed, he started writing under the name of Dermot O'Byrne. (His autobiography *Farewell My Youth* [1943], which covers the period to the time of the First World War, is an immensely enjoyable one.) After reading Yeats's *The Wanderings of Oisin*, Bax virtually trained himself to "become" Irish, and based one of his tone poems (a genre that particularly suited him), *In the Faery Hills* (1909), on Yeats's work. Over and above the Celtic dream world of legends, further spice was added to Bax's mental and emotional makeup in the form of Russian musical influences that stemmed from his visit to the Ukraine in pursuit of a young woman in 1910. The Lisztian Piano Sonata No. 1 (1910), piano pieces such as the two *Russian Tone-Pictures* (*May Night in the Ukraine* and *Gopak* [1911]), and *In a Vodka Shop* (1915)—even the incidental music for Barrie's play, *The Truth About the Russian Dancer* (1920)—all give evidence of the considerable impact his journey to Russia had made on him.

Bax, not unlike Delius, was susceptible to approaching music via some program, literary or otherwise, which he then translated into music. Thus the extramusical ideas in Bax's music are metamorphosed into the language of sound.

Today, apart from his symphonic poem *The Garden of Fand* (1913–16), based on an Irish legend, hardly any work of his is known by the public. Yet, like Sibelius, he too composed seven remarkable symphonies between 1921 and 1939 in an unashamedly romantic and highly personal idiom. These, like several of his other compositions, including some of his concertos, notably the Violin Concerto (1938) and the *Concertante* (1938–39) for piano left hand, are awaiting rediscovery. There is enough greatness in Bax's music to survive a period of neglect.

John Ireland (1879–1962)

It is significant that Bax dedicated his Symphony No. 1 (1921) to his friend John Ireland, for Ireland shared his romantic spirit and vision. Although Ireland did not compose symphonies, as he believed that, apart from Elgar's two symphonies, the British contribution to this form was "poppycock," his contribution to the orchestral repertoire is proof of his versatility. He wrote tone poems, such as *The Forgotten Rite Prelude* (1913), overtures, like *A London Overture* (1936), suites, such as the *Downland Suite* for brass band (1932), and the Piano Concerto (1930) in which classical form, Lisztian thematic procedure and jazzy sound effects blend in well with an essentially romantic lyricism.

Apart from his romanticism, Ireland had an affinity with particular places—above all the Channel Islands. For him, this empathy became something of an equivalent to Bax's Celtic revelation. Several of his compositions were inspired by this sense of attachment. The aforementioned *The Forgotten Rite Prelude* and the syphonic rhapsody *Mai-Dun* (1920–21) and the piano pieces *The Island Spell* (1921) and *Sarnia (An Island Sequence)* (1940–41) all illustrate how fruitful an impact this relationship had on Ireland.

His musical style is characterised by a strong Brahmsian influence and is further marked by the intoxicating influence of Debussy and Stravinsky. The result is that his chamber music and piano compositions in particular are distinguished lyrical additions to British music. Outstanding examples of his chamber works are the Cello Sonata (1923) and the *Fantasy Sonata* (1943) for clarinet; these and the *Ballade of London Nights* (1929; published 1968) clearly indicate the provenance of his style.

By now, however, thanks to a better historical perspective, it is Ireland's songs, such as the settings of six Housman poems under the title *The Land of Lost Content* (1920–21) and the Thomas Hardy poems, *Three Hardy Songs* (1925) and *Five Poems by Thomas Hardy* (1926), that strike one as being his best accomplishment and most significant contribution. In all of them English restraint and French sensibility, as learned from Gabriel Fauré and Debussy, are cross-fertilised in a highly personal way.

2

The Folk Song Revival and Its Influence:
Cecil Sharp, Ralph Vaughan Williams,
Gustav Holst, George Butterworth

> If I may venture to give my own definition of folk song, I
> should call it "an individual flowering on a common stem."
> —Vaughan Williams

A characteristic and indeed inevitable feature of nationalism, whether nineteenth-century or otherwise, is the need to search for origins of what can be perceived as the natural voice of a country, its unmistakable sound-profile, as it were, in terms of music. In such a search for national identity, whether in Russia, the countries of central Europe, Scandinavia, or Spain, the tendency has been to turn to folk—that is, peasant—tradition, as well as to the past. In the nineteenth century, the emphatic cultivation and projection of these two elements, in which a nation can rediscover and emphasise with pride values that have hitherto been buried, and which are then revived and used as foundation stones in order to build up an independent socio-political or cultural profile, happened in a striking way. England, of course, did not have territorial problems or problems of national identity. On the contrary, she was at the very height of her power and sense of self-assurance. The problem that she shared with Russia, middle Europe, and elsewhere was that, in musical matters, she was largely under Austro-German domination, influenced by the language and tradition of Bach, Haydn, Mozart, Beethoven, Brahms, Wagner, and others. A strong desire to break away from this German musical hegemony and to create in its place an indigenous

23

English musical language was the aim of several great personalities at the turn of the century.

Cecil Sharp (1859–1924)

One of the leading figures in fostering the cause of folk song and folk dance revival was Cecil Sharp. The effects of his dedicated research and, above all, of the enthusiastic vision with which he set out to propagate his findings for the benefit of his country can hardly be overstated. His impact on creative musicians such as Holst, Vaughan Williams, and Butterworth was substantial. He stands as one of the great generating forces behind the emancipation of English music from German domination, and, as such, he made a major contribution to the development of the Second English Renaissance in music. A Londoner, he studied law and music and then went to Australia, where he practised law as well as music. He became an organist of the cathedral at Adelaide and, while there, found time to establish a music school. On his return to England, he was appointed principal of the Hampstead Conservatoire, a post which he held from 1896 to 1905. During this period he became involved with folk dancing, having been inspired by seeing Morris dancing in Oxfordshire. His interest naturally led him to recognise the significance of folk music as the very foundation of national art.

With zealousness comparable to that of Bartók and Kodály in Hungary, he set out to collect folk songs and dances. He joined the Folk Song Society, founded in 1898, and was to have a lasting influence upon its activities. He collected well over four thousand tunes, if his American collections are included in the total. His publications of these, such as the series of *Folk-songs from Somerset* (produced in collaboration with C. L. Marson, 1904–9), *The Country Dance Book* (with Butterworth and Karpeles, 1909–22), *English Folk Carols* (1911), *English Folk-songs from the South Appalachian mountains* (1917), *A Collection of Selected Folk-songs* (with Vaughan Williams, 1918), and several didactic publications that he wrote in order to make folk songs familiar in schools, demonstrate his total dedication to the genre. One of his most important books, which should be made a regular feature of English and music studies because of its nobility of thought and vision, is *English Folk-song: Some Conclusions* (1907). In this remarkable study, his love of his country's folk music reaches the realm of the universal. "Folk music," he wrote, "is the ungarbled and ingenious expression of the human mind and on that account it must reflect the essential and basic qualities of the human mind."

In order to balance the work of the Folk Song Society he founded the English Folk Dance Society in 1911. After his death, these two societies were eventually joined under the same roof in Cecil Sharp House, London. At the time of his death he was engaged on translating Arbeau's *Orchesographie* (1589), a classical collection of dances from the late Middle Ages and Renaissance, with fine choreographical illustrations to its revealing text.

Ralph Vaughan Williams (1872–1958)

The influence of the folk music revival had a liberating effect on music in England, giving a new impetus to several composers who were in search of their own musical identity. One of the most endearing of these figures was Ralph Vaughan Williams. During his long life span, backed by the financial security of a private income, he developed as a composer at a steady, comfortable pace, as though he had eternity in front of him—and, in a way, he had. As a student, he attended the Cambridge University and the Royal College of Music. He had many eminent teachers, including Parry and Stanford in England and Bruch in Berlin and Ravel in Paris. His composing evolved from a complex mix of influences: from German and contemporary English music, as well as from the last of the great English composers before Elgar, Henry Purcell; from his deep understanding of the Tudor composers; from folk music, which he started collecting in 1902; and from his work as the editor of the *English Hymnal* (1906). The folk element is very marked. His harmonic thinking is more profoundly rooted in the largely modal world of folk music, old hymn tunes, and Renaissance music than shaped by the influence of the French music he learned from Ravel. In any case, the three months he spent studying with Ravel in 1908 could not have given more than a final touch to something that was already slowly materializing in him.

But in fairness to Ravel, it is true that, on returning to England after his period of study with him, Vaughan Williams gave free rein to his creativity in a series of major compositions. It is as though Ravel had helped him to find his voice.

The imagery of the sea is naturally a frequently used subject in English arts, above all in painting and music. Turner, one of the great painters of the nineteenth century, was obsessed with it. Among musicians, the list of names and works is impressive: Stanford's *Songs of the Sea,* op. 91 (1904), Elgar's *Sea Pictures,* op. 37 (1897–99), Delius's *Sea Drift* (1903–4), and Bax's *The Garden of Fand* (1913) are some outstanding examples of the stimulating effect of the sea. It is not surprising that one of Vaughan Williams's firt large-scale compositions was his *Sea Symphony* (1906–9).

Like Delius, he admired the poems of Whitman. Unlike Delius, however, who gave emphasis to egocentric nostalgia, Vaughan Williams emphasized the humanistic vision inherent in "A Song for all Seas, all Ships," as well as seeking out the daring spirit of exploration. Superficially, the traditional plan of four movements in the *Sea Symphony* invites listeners to interpret it as a symphony with soloists and chorus in the style of the Finale of Beethoven's Symphony No. 9. In reality, however, one is confronted with an ingenious amalgamation of the oratorio so much liked in England, the romantic orchestrated songs as practised by Brahms and Mahler, and, for good measure, a classical symphonic structure. All in all, in spite of its impurity, the *Sea Symphony* is a lovable musical mongrel.

From the time of his association with Sharp and Holst, and above all, once he began his own folk song collecting, the direct influence of folk music became evident in several of Vaughan Williams's compositions, notably in *Three Norfolk Rhapsodies* (1905–6), *Five English Folk-songs* (1913), *Fantasia on "Greensleeves"* (1934), and numerous arrangements of folk songs and carols. But the most striking manifestation of Vaughan Williams's ability to absorb English folk music and make it part of his own musical idiom was not so much his use of actual folk melodies, but his capacity to make musical statements that sound as if they are of folk origin. According to Bartók, this is the ultimate accomplishment in assimilating folk music. Many such examples can be found in Vaughan Williams's music from *In the Fen Country* (1904) onwards. It is also evident in his settings of poetry, especially of Barnes's *Linden Lea* (1901), Stevenson's *Songs of Travel* (1905), and Housman's *On Wenlock Edge* from *A Shropshire Lad* (1908–9). In these compositions his inspiration ascends towards Schubertian levels of perfection. In Vaughan Williams's last song settings, the Austro-German *Lied* is metamorphosed and gains an authentic English mode of expression by virtue of being founded on native musical idiom. The dates of the two song cycles mentioned above are telling, since they correspond to Vaughan Williams's most intense involvement with folk music and the *English Hymnal*.

Another aspect of his musical idiom, the lyrical pastoral style, which dominated the whole of the British musical scene between the two world wars and beyond, up to the 1950s, is similarly based not only on his personal temperament but also on the nature of English folk music itself. Folk music also gave him a strong sense of modality, and his modal thinking was further influenced by his study of Tudor music and by some French music, notably that of Fauré, Debussy, and Ravel, as his String Quartet No. 1 (1908) shows. Equally important as an influence was the frequent use of compound meters in English folk music. It is interesting to note that Elgar, who had nothing to do with the folk music movement, used a compound meter in a strikingly lyrical, pastoral manner, for example, in the first movement of his Cello Concerto. This suggests that the mellow, undulating English landscape and the pastoral mood evoked by compound meters are perhaps essential elements in the English collective subconscious—and very likely reflected in the rhythmic patterns of language as well. (By comparison, in Hungary, where folk music has had a comparable impact on musical awakening and where the accent in speech falls on the first syllable, giving it a metric and staccato effect, compound meters in music are relatively rare.) The pastoral mood is, of course, not bound up with being a countryman; it is more an attitude of mind. Peasants, by and large, do not relate to the countryside in a pastoral mood—artists, however, largely do.

Both the quality and the extensive range of Vaughan Williams's repertoire demonstrate that his place in the history of English music is seminal. His works cover a wide range of musical forms. His massive contribution to the English symphonic repertoire is based on nine symphonies, of which numbers 4, 5, and 6 (first performed 1935, 1943, and 1948, respectively) are perhaps his most impressive creations in this genre. The Epilogue of his Symphony No. 6 is one of the great slow movements of this century. In it, a strange modal world gives expression to a sadness that is reminiscent of the desolate foreboding atmosphere of Wagner's opening of the third act of *Tristan*.

His other orchestral works are no less impressive: the famous *Fantasia on a Theme by Thomas Tallis* (1910) (see chapter 3, p. 38), his concertos, including a Romance (1952) for harmonica and a Tuba Concerto (1954), as well as his numerous scores for film music, as for instance, *Scott of the Antarctic* (1947–48) and the *Vision of William Blake* (1957), are all examples of his versatility. But it is in his choral compositions that his typical warmth seems to come increasingly to the fore. In these—disliked by some for their hybrid nature, but loved by others because of their humanistic vision—he shakes hands, as it were with the English choral tradition, as, for example, in *Five Tudor Portraits* (1935), *Dona nobis pacem* (1936), and *Serenade to Music* (1938).

His operas are nowadays seldom performed, although *The Pilgrim's Progress* (composed between 1906 and 1951), based on Bunyan's allegory, is interesting because it represents an attempt to blend the forms of opera and morality play. He even wrote ballet scores, one of which, *Job, a Masque for Dancing* (1927–30), based on Blake's illustrations to the Book of Job, is among his greatest compositions (why it is seldom performed is a mystery that only the entrepreneurs of the performing arts can explain). During his long life he managed to weave together dissimilar threads of both continental and English musical traditions, out of which he created a tapestry of sounds that is nevertheless singularly English. The Constable-like musical tableaux of decency and sensibility and the fine sentiments that backed the vision of humanity that characterizes the best of his works are nowadays sometimes frowned at and condemned as tweedy and parochial. This may occasionally be so, yet his music, like good company, ennobles.

Gustav Holst (1874–1934)

Holst was a great friend of Vaughan Williams, and, like him, he was interested in the folk music movement and in Tudor music.

His music, however, was less deeply affected by the movement of the folk song revival. Born at Cheltenham into a family of musicians of Swedish descent, Holst learned early to play the violin, piano, and organ, to which he later added the trombone and also conducting. But his main interest from his teens was composition. His early compositions show the influence of German romanticism, above all, that of Wagner whose phenomenal impact hardly anyone could avoid. He also shared with Delius and Vaughan Williams a literary fascination with Whitman's poetry. *The Mystic Trumpeter,* op. 18 (1904), for soprano and orchestra, for example, is a setting of a Whitman text. Holst had a searching, perhaps restless, and definitely intense mind, a liberal taste, and a natural leaning toward Eastern mysticism. His involvement with Eastern philosophy and Sanskrit literature, which he learned with determination, is reflected in the choice of subject for several of his compositions—for examples, *Savitri,* op. 25 (1908), an opera *di camera,* taken from a Sanskrit text; *Three Choral Hymns,* op. 26 (1908–10), from the *Rig Veda;* the *Oriental Suite "Beni Mora,"* op. 29 (1910), influenced by a visit to Algeria. Moreover, his interest in Fabian socialism and in the ideas of William Morris, combined with his total dedication to practical music-making in the service of the community, led him to conduct the Socialist Choir and to a lifelong involvement with teaching. In 1907, he became the Music Director of Morley College; this was in addition to other teaching commitments, of which the most striking and time-consuming was his appointment as Director of Music at St. Paul's Girls School, London. There, in spite of poor health, he served the cause of music with enthusiasm from 1905 until his death in 1934.

The effect of his friendships with Sharp and Vaughan Williams, who fostered his growing interest in folk music and his movement away from Teutonic musical influences, gained expression in his *A Somerset Rhapsody* (1906–7). Appropriately he dedicated this to Cecil Sharp who had collected the songs used by Holst. It is an evocative and delightful work that has withstood the test of time and belongs to a distinguished array of kindred compositions written by Vaughan Williams, Kodály, and Bartók. His relationship with the St. Paul's Girls School bore fruit with his *St. Paul's Suite* (1913) for string orchestra and the *Brook Green Suite* (named after the address of the school) (1933), in which actual folk song and folk song influences are clearly evident. Another apparent folk music influence on Holst's thinking is displayed in his partiality for asymmetric or "Bulgarian" rhythm, that is $\frac{5}{4}$ and $\frac{7}{4}$. The influence of Oriental and Arabic music and, above all, the music of Stravinsky—who left a deep impression on him—should also be noted.

Even today, Holst is still largely remembered by the general public for one piece only: his most effective *The Planets*, op. 32 (1914–17), a suite for orchestra. As the title suggests, the seven movements in it are astrological characterisations, as, for example: No. 1, "Mars, the Bringer of War"; No. 4, "Jupiter, the Bringer of Jollity"; and No. 7, "Neptune, the Mystic" (this latter movement utilizes a wordless female choir—a musical feature then much in vogue). *The Planets*, however, is only one aspect of Holst's genius. A less popular but much more fascinating side of him was his mystical introversion; this was given expression in some exquisite, truly idiosyncratic Holstian sound effects, as, for example, in his tone poems *Egdon Heath*, op. 47 (1927), inspired by Thomas Hardy's description of a stretch of countryside in Dorset, and *Hammersmith: Prelude and Scherzo for Orchestra*, op. 52 (1930–31), a mysterious, highly personal evocation of a part of London. Musicians, like painters, have reacted not only to rural but also to urban topics and districts. Certain parts of London, for example, have been more favored than others, and Hammersmith was such a district. The English painter Victor Pasmore painted *The Hanging Gardens of Hammersmith No. 1* during the Second World War. The quasi-mystical, subdued atmosphere created in the painting is, in pictorial terms, not unlike Holst's own tone poem composed fourteen years earlier.

With his *A Fugal Overture*, op. 40, no. 1 (1922), and *Fugal Concerto*, op. 40, no. 2 (1923), Holst was among the first to parallel the continental "Back to Bach" or neoclassical movement, a trend that evolved during the 1920s largely under the leadership of Stravinsky. Holst's path was, in many ways, an innovative one, and it has only been through the help of many friends and, above all, through the unfailing dedicated help of his daughter, Imogen Holst, who spent her life promoting her father's music, that his work is now steadily gaining the recognition it deserves. Certainly, of the three masters, Elgar, Delius, and Holst, who died in the same year—1934—it was Holst who produced music that most closely belongs to the twentieth century.

George Butterworth (1885–1916)

Butterworth had one of those backgrounds which fits the stereotyped image of the English educated class. Son of Sir Alexander Kaye Butterworth and grandson of John Kaye, bishop of Lincoln, he went to Eton as a King's Scholar and then to Trinity College, Oxford. He also studied for a short while at the Royal College of Music. Then, in search of professional direction, he turned to music criticism and joined the staff of *The Times* newspaper. Dissatisfied, he tried his hand at teaching—at Radley College in Oxfordshire. Having developed an interest in folk music and folk dancing as an undergraduate at Oxford, he now began collecting folk songs. His interest in the folk song revival led him to meet and establish friendships with Sharp and Vaughan Williams; it was encountering and absorbing the nature of English folk music that inspired Butterworth's compositional thinking. His own collection and arrangement of the *Eleven Folk-songs from Sussex* (1911) illustrate that, whereas Sharp's own arrangements of folk songs are often superimpositions rooted in the style of Victorian song accompaniment, both Vaughan Williams's and Butterworth's accompaniments grow out of the very nature of the songs; their harmonic understanding was superior to Sharp's.

The few compositions that he had a chance to write before his early death illustrate the spiritual integrity of a budding genius. His small and sensitively lyrical compositions, characterised by a directness learned from folk song, number about a dozen in all. His reputation rests on even less, but the six songs from *A Shropshire Lad* (1911) on the poems of Housman, *"A Shropshire Lad"*: *Rhapsody for Orchestra* (1912), and *"The Banks of Green Willow"*: *Idyll for Small Orchestra* (1913) are pearls in the history of English music.

At the outbreak of the First World War in 1914, he, like so many, enlisted with enthusiasm, as if finding some purpose in life at the very moment when life was to be negated on a horrifying scale. He was valiant and, for his brave defence of a trench, was awarded the Military Cross, which he never had the pleasure of receiving as he was killed in action at the battle of the Somme. His loss to music is comparable with the loss to literature of the poets Rupert Brooke and Wilfred Owen.

3

The Past into the Present: Folk Music, the English Carol, the Choral Tradition, the Beginning of Musical Scholarship, Impressionism

> If you are going to have a big foot in the future, you've got to have a big foot in the past.
>
> —Luka Foss

In the previous chapter, it has been argued that the search for national identity in music during the nineteenth and early twentieth centuries tended in two distinct directions: study of folk music and reappraisal of the past. These aspects of the musical revival in Britain will now be discussed in more detail.

Folk Music

The folk music revival came in the nick of time. The avalanche of the industrial revolution was about to destroy the last traces of real folk music, which is based on the orally transmitted traditions of country people and on agriculturally centered values. In more than one sense the preservation of folk music is therefore closely linked with the past, as folk music is deeply rooted in the collective heritage of a country. Indeed, the origin of many folk songs collected during the nineteenth and early twentieth centuries goes back to much earlier periods. They represent a continuous link between past and present that no nation can afford to sever. On the other hand, of course, an ideologically geared overemphasis on folklore can easily deteriorate into parochialism. Folk songs

33

are too precious to be cheapened by politically oriented populari-
zation, either class based or jingoistic.

The English Carol

Another development that took place at the same time as the
folk song revival, and which in a way is related to it, was the revival
of the rich tradition of the English carol. Carols dating back to the
fifteenth century (for example, the *Coventry Carol*) were originally
round dances—festive processional compositions—that eventually
evolved into songs. The texts of these carols might have been expected to deal with such subjects as the birth of Jesus, Bethlehem,
or the Three Kings. But this was not always so, as several of the
carols are adaptations from texts of pagan origin. This dual background reveals itself in hybrid imageries, as in the text of perhaps
the most popular carol of all "The Holly and the Ivy," which was
collected by Sharp in Gloucestershire. Both the Reformation and
the industrial revolution had adverse effects on the fate of this
form of traditional singing. The Reformation frowned, to say the
least, on the cult of the Virgin birth, as well as on music, and its
concerns are well illustrated in an act of Parliament of 1642:

> If any person or persons . . . commonly called Fidlers or Minstrels
> shall be taken playing, fidling, or making music, in any Inn, Alehouse,
> or Tavern—or shall be taken intreating any person . . . to hear them
> play . . . that every such person shall be adjudged rogues, vagabounds,
> and sturdy beggars . . . and be punished as such.[1]

Those involved with the industrial revolution were not in the least
disturbed about the destruction of the national heritage. The miracle, showing the conservative resilience of the British people, is
that in spite of such devastations so much has been preserved.

The salvaging of some of the carols was undertaken as early as
1822 by Dr. Gilbert and W. Sandys, who published two modest
collections. Once interest in carols was regained, more collections
followed. From the publication of *Carols for Christmastide* by the
Revds. T. Holmore and J. Neale (1853) through *English Folk Carols*
(1911) by Cecil Sharp, to *The Penguin Book of Christmas Carols* by
E. Poston (1965), the list of carol editing and publishing is impres-

sive. It should be stressed that all carols are by no means of folk origin; their popularity and long history, however, secure them a place next to folk songs, as they represent an almost unbroken popular tradition from the Middle Ages to the present. As in the case of folk songs, the revival of carols made an impression on several English composers who put them to good use in their compositions—sometimes to brilliant effect. Two outstanding examples are the *Fantasia on Christmas Carols* (1912) by Vaughan Williams, and the *Ceremony of Carols,* op. 28 (1942) by Benjamin Britten. The annual carol service broadcast on Christmas Eve from King's College, Cambridge, has become an established part of national Christmas celebrations.

The Choral Tradition

For the sake of convenience, the English choral tradition can be divided into three main periods: from Middle Ages to the end of the seventeenth century (to Purcell), from Handel to the late Victorian period, and, lastly, from the beginning of the twentieth century. Some critics may, of course, justifiably argue that Handel was a glorious episode, an imported extension of Purcell, or that the whole of Victorian English choral activities were Brahms- and Mendelssohn-oriented and a vainglorious and sentimental aping of Handel giving rise to the notion of the English "Messiah-complex." Furthermore, it could be argued, as Peter Pirie does in his book *The English Musical Renaissance,* that:

> The nineteenth-century choral movement started as a social rather than an artistic phenomenon; it was a conscientious attempt to improve the morality of the workers of the Industrial Revolution, whose condition was rapidly sinking into the enormous wretchedness depicted with such sombre power by the drawings of Victorian London by Gustave Doré.[2]

The spreading of the tonic sol-fa method under its instigator, John Curwen, the founder of the Tonic Sol-fa Association as well as of the publishing firm Curwen and Sons, seems to bear out Pirie's interpretation.

The striking fact, however, is that, regardless of artistic quality,

the only unbroken musical tradition that carried on in England
during its musical "dark age" was a predeliction for singing, in
the form of singing hymn tunes and traditional songs or in under-
taking various choral music activites including madrigal singing,
a tradition maintained by societies such as the Madrigal Society
of London, founded as early as 1741. These activities should by
no means be belittled, as they have served not only to maintain
live music-making, but also to foster the composing of outstanding
choral music from Elgar to the present. It is little known in Great
Britain that the Kodály Music Method, which has revolutionised
Hungarian musical education, is directly indebted to the English
choral singing tradition, a tradition that impressed Kodály during
his visit to England in 1927. In an interview, in December 1962,
Kodály spoke about the development of music teaching in Hungary, and added:

> I have collected the choral themes for school use from among the
> pearls of the thesaurus of Hungarian folk-songs. These themes, by
> the way, have spread beyond the frontiers of Hungary. It is an interest-
> ing fact—although it's not just by chance—that they will become the
> common treasure of teachers and children in a country whose musical
> culture has inspired me many times during my life. That country is
> Britain, where I had the opportunity to study the teaching of singing
> at schools in 1927. I was able then to get acquainted with those British
> composers and musicologists who, simultaneously with, but wholly
> independently from us, followed a similar course in their folk-song re-
> search.[3]

Kodály's manner of linking up singing, teaching, and folk music
research demonstrates a parallel between the two countries' remarkable developments in music during the course of the twentieth century.

The Beginnings of Musical Scholarship

Another invigorating cultural tonic given to English music during the nineteenth century was the development of musical scholarship. This led to the reevaluation of the musical past, the
studying of English musical ancestry. This in turn encouraged
for publication and eventual performance of the works of nearly
forgotten masters from the Middle Ages to Purcell's time.
Learned societies, such as the Musical Antiquarian Society, were

founded with subscriptions enabling the members to purchase the numerous volumes containing the music of composers, as well as popular tunes, of earlier times. Mendelssohn, the darling of Victorian England, gave a historic performance of Bach's *St Matthew Passion* in 1829, thus inaugurating the "rediscovery" of Bach, whose work had lain neglected for three generations, surviving often only in manuscript form, and so beginning the Bach cult in Europe. Mirroring many revivalist societies abroad, the English Bach Society was founded in 1849. Thus scholarship, the taste for revivalism, and the activity of enlightened publishers—of whom W. Chappell stands out—together with the English fondness for clubs and societies, all seem to have been synchronized at the right time to bring about a far-reaching reappraisal of things past. The list of publications during the nineteenth and early twentieth centuries encompasses works from John Dunstable, who was one of the most influential composers of his time, through Tudor church composers and the English madrigalists—such as Taverner, Tallis, Byrd, Gibbons, and Morley—to Purcell's work. Many contributed—and are still contributing—to this healthy vogue for revivalism backed by scholarship. Perhaps one of the major figures was the musicologist E. H. Fellowes, whose interest in the music of the Tudor period culminated in the massive tasks of editing the *English Madrigal School* in thirty-six volumes, the *English School of Lutenist Song-Writers,* the works of William Byrd in twenty volumes, as well as books on Byrd and Gibbons.

Many English composers have found the encounter with the great musical past of English music a revelation. Like the impact of folk music, it has given further impetus to the formulating of their own musical language by enriching it and linking it up with a musical heritage to which they can relate with dignity. By absorbing their natural musical past, English composers have regained their confidence and feel part of a musical nation again. Frank Howes, whose prejudices ran in favor of the folk school but who was one of the most perceptive writers on English music, asked in connection with Cecil Sharp:

Was there not something symbolical in the fact that his first song, redolent of English flowers, was collected in a village rectory garden, from a man whose name was John England, in the first years of new century (1903 to be precise)? This song was "The Seeds of Love."[4]

Equally significant is the fact that soon after, in 1910, Vaughan Williams's *Fantasia on a Theme by Thomas Tallis* for double string orchestra was given its first performance. (The theme is the third of the nine Psalms that Tallis wrote for Archbishop Parker in 1567.) With it, an antiphonal modal world was evoked in the twentieth century, which, while being a homage to the past, introduced an authentically English musical style. If, within the context of the history of English music, Elgar's *Enigma Variations* is a milestone at the last phase of romanticism, then Vaughan Williams's *Fantasia* is a milestone at the beginning of the twentieth century.

Impressionism

In general parlance musical impressionism is usually equated with modernism, and with good reason. Yet in reality the problem is much more complex, as the impressionistic style in music is not only related to romanticism in general, and rooted in Wagner's music and theories in particular, but also, even more significantly, relies heavily on potpourri of medieval practice (parallel organum), Renaissance vocal style (chanson), and the programmatic keyboard style of such late seventeenth- and eighteenth-century French composers as Couperin and Rameau. To all these, the sounds of Russia (Mussorgsky) and Far-Eastern music (Gamelan) together with Mediterranean—largely Iberian Latin/Moorish— exoticism should be added for good measure. Debussy is largely associated with impressionism in music, notwithstanding the fact that he did not like to be classified as an impressionist. His influence was, of course, immense. Modernism without him can hardly be comprehended. As far as the English composers at the turn of the century and beyond are concerned, it is apparent that his influence was as much due to his success in breaking away from the German musical hegemony—largely by amalgamating styles from the French musical past—as to the "modern" effects in his music.

Delius is often referred to as the "English Debussy," with some justification. Both shared a love of nature, a programmatic approach to music, and an exceptional sensitivity to orchestral color. Both created improvisationlike shifting of sounds and a marked sensuality, although in Delius this tends to be subjective, whereas in Debussy the impression given is of detachment and cool observation. The best examples of Delius's impressionistic style are, of course, *In a Summer Garden: Rhapsody for Orchestra* (1908), *Summer Night on the River* (1911), and the *North Country Sketches* (1913–14).

Bax's music, by its association with the Irish poet W. B. Yeats, who in turn was influenced by the symbolists, among them Maeterlinck, shows the effect of impressionism in *The Garden of Fand* (1913–16) and *Tintagel* (1917) among other compositions in which he gave poetic expression to the dreamworld of Celtic twilight. John Ireland, too, displays a profound assimilation of the music of both Debaussy and Ravel, especially in such piano works as *Decorations* (1912–13). Holst's predilection with Oriental mysticism blends in well with the impressionist/symbolist style, especially in "Nepture, the Mystic" from *The Planets*, in which a wordless choir adds to the evocation of infinite remoteness. Vaughan Williams, perhaps even more than other English composers, shows a pronounced influence of impressionism in his music, but with a different emphasis. Whereas one of the most obvious attractions of the impressionist style is color, that is, effects of instrumentation tending towards the "plein air" in music, he ingeniously absorbed the harmonic implications of the French impressionists and amalgamated them with the English world of Tudor music, Purcell, the hymn, and the tradition of folk song. Therein lies an answer to the question of how, in spite of the fact that both Debussy and Vaughan Williams are largely evocative composers often using similar compositional techniques, Debussy is always French and Vaughan Williams unmistakably English. A personal version of impressionism peremates many of Vaughan Williams's compositions, most strikingly his orchestral works, as, for example, his *London Symphony* (1911–14) and *Pastoral Symphony* (1916–21). In these works, his fundamentally romantic temperament, relying on the framework of the Austro-German symphonic tradition, is enriched by the shimmering nuances of impressionist tone-paintings and English and continental harmonic vocabularies, giving a strange combination of succulent austerity.

For obvious reasons, discussion here has been restricted to the effect of impressionism on a selection of composers from Delius to Vaughan Williams. The impact of impressionism in all the arts, however, continues to affect us strongly.

4

Modernists in the Making:
Frank Bridge, Arthur Bliss,
William Walton, Constant Lambert

Nothing matures or grows old more rapidly than music. The brilliant audacity of one generation declines into the sober commonplace of another.

—Sir Thomas Beecham

In their heyday the four composers to be discussed in this chapter gave the impression of being in the vanguard of modern developments in music. By now, from a more distant perspective, their position seems to be much less radical—indeed, in the case of Walton, for example, it is moderate, if not conservative.

Frank Bridge (1879–1941)

Like so many English composers, Bridge was a pupil of Sir Charles Villiers Stanford. He became an accomplished all-around musician, who, as a violin and viola player for many years, played in what were then well-known string quartets, like the Grimson, Joachim, and English quartets. Although he composed several excellent orchestral works, such as *The Sea* (1910–11), a suite for orchestra, and *Oration, Concerto elegiaco* (1930) for cello and orchestra, his main contribution to twentieth-century English music is his chamber music. He was also a capable conductor, perhaps taking after his father who was conductor of the Brighton Theatre Orchestra: indeed, he was good enough to deputize for the conductor and founder of the Promenade Concerts, Henry Wood—by no means a small achievement. As a composer, his technique evolved via a long journey from Brahms and Stanford to the masters of the Second Viennese School—Schoenberg, Berg, and Webern. It is significant that of the three, the most lyrical, Alban Berg, was his favorite. His early compositions show the influences of the Austro-German romantic style and, of course, of his teacher Stanford, as, for example, in his *Bologna String Quartet* (1906) and *Phantasie Piano Quartet* (1910). Bridge's attraction to a quasi-cyclic structure, in his case the reintroduction of an earlier theme or themes in the Finale, thereby achieving emotional and structural unity, is already apparent in his *Bologna String Quartet.* *Summer* (1914), an orchestral tone poem, shows the direct influence of Delius. At that time Bridge was maturing into a composer who seemed to be destined to be a link between Delius and Vaughan Williams: he displayed a gently pastoral style, but without a trace of folk music influence. This, however, was not the way things turned out, as, from around 1920, he modified his style. He started to write more modern music, largely influenced by the German modernists of the time. This change in style is apparent from his Piano Sonata (1921–24) onwards, and it gained mature expression in his last two string quartets (no. 3, 1926, and no. 4, 1937), the Violin Sonata (1932), and strange, short work, *Divertimenti* (1934–38) for four woodwind instruments.

His modernism, however, was as far from the real thing as the late Beethoven *Bagatelles* are from, say, Webern's *Six Bagatelles.* That is to say, the superficial similarities (the concentration of musical thought finding an outlet in minimalistic utterances, as in *Divertimenti*) are counterbalanced, if not undermined, by the tonality-fixed romantic temperament. Yet there was a price to pay for his modest modernism, and that was neglect. His comeback, if it has occurred at all, has been rathe slow. Nowadays the general public remembers him chiefly for a couple of fine songs, *Go Not Happy Day* and *Love Went A-Riding*, and for his happy relationship with Benjamin Britten, who was his pupil and who guaranteed him a place in posterity, at least, in his own composition, the *Variations on a Theme of Frank Bridge*, op. 10 (1937).

Sir Arthur Bliss (1891–1975)

Of American descent, Bliss was also a pupil of Stanford, but whereas most English composers of the period emerged out of late romanticism and out of Elgar's style, as it were, he did the reverse. After returning from the war in 1919, he astonished the musical scene with his cosmopolitan savoir faire. He started as an *enfant terrible* and then retreated into an Elgar-influenced romantic heartiness—a style particularly suited to film music and to his being Master of the Queen's Music.

His early works correspond to and were influenced by the French avant-garde: Ravel and the members of *Les Six*, together with Stravinsky and even jazz. The solo songs with ensembles, *Madame Noy* (1918), *Rhapsody* (1919), and *Rout* (1920), the song cycle *The Women of Yueh* (1923), and *Mêlée fantasque* for orchestra (1921) show wit and an experimental spirit, reflecting the style of the frivolous twentieth century with nonsense syllables and all. But beginning with his *Colour Symphony* (1921–22), in which the colors purple, red, blue, and green appearing in heraldry gain musical expression, he adopted—via neoclassical preoccupations, in vogue from the 1920s to the late 1940—a style that offers a middle course between Elgar and Walton. His neoclassicism is made self-evident in his *Music for Strings* (1935), as it is in the line of Bach's *Brandenburg Concertos* and Elgar's *Introduction and Allegro*. Like Vaughan Williams, Bliss also paid homage to the past in such works as his *Purcell Suite* (1921) and, particularly, his *Meditations on a Theme of John Blow* (1955). He had a natural sense of the extremely grandiose and a panache for quickly assimilating modern musical trends that he then transformed for his own good use.

In a way, listening to his music is also a didactic experience, because he was, perhaps unwittingly, a popularizer of modernism in England by virtue of the fact that he diluted it with easily palatable romantic flavors. The Piano Concerto (1938) is a good example; It mixes the style of the brilliant romantic concertos of Liszt, Tchaikovsky, and Rachmaninov with the Elgar of the *Pomp and Circumstances Marches* and also has a touch of Waltonic modernism just to bring it painlessly up to date. Bliss's music seldom plumbs real depths, as the sense of tragedy, which is an essential ingredient in the alchemy of a really great artist, seems to have been entirely missing from his temperament and thought. He was a happy and fortunate man whose complacency is somewhat apparent in his music. It is revealing that he excelled as a ballet and film music composer. Indeed, apart from his *Colour Symphony*, he is largely remembered by the general public for his ballet *Checkmate* (1937) and for some brilliant film scores: *Things to Come* (1934–35, from H. G. Wells's book *The Shape of Things to Come*) and *Conquest of the Air* (1937), to mention only two. His versatile talent covered a wide range of compositional forms, including an opera, *The Olympians* (1948–49), set to a libretto by J. B. Priestley, and some instrumental music, the writing of which was often triggered by encounters with outstanding performers, such as Goossens, Solomon, and Rostropovich. His autobiography *As I Remember* (1970) reveals the sort of man he was, kind and generous, interested in the arts and artists (Epstein, Hepworth, and Nicholson were among his friends), an immensely capable and contented being. In all, a great talent and a good man, but lacking that hardly explicable extra dimension which makes a genius.

Sir William Walton (1902–83)

Walton was the son of a choirmaster and singing teacher. His good voice enabled him to become a chorister at Christ Church Cathedral, Oxford, at the age of ten. In his late teens he became a protégé of the literary Sitwell siblings, Osbert, Sacheverell, and Edith. For a while he even lived with them as a quasi-"adopted brother" in London and Italy. With this entrée into the artistic world of London and beyond, Walton was more or less launched both artistically and socially.

He started as a well-looked-after *enfant terrible*, but his modernism, not unlike Bliss's, was a flash in the pan, and it was not sustained. His first international appearance as a composer was in 1923 with a string quartet that was performed at the International Society for Contemporary Music in Salzburg. The totally unknown young English composer, without any formal teaching and a pupil of no one, was offering an atonal work. According to Sitwell, Alban Berg was sufficiently impressed by Walton's String Quartet to refer to him as "the leader of English atonal music." Later Walton withdrew this work, his first avant-garde essay in this genre. But what did create a scandal, bringing Walton's name to public attention, was the first public performance in 1923 (there was a private one in 1922) of *Façade* (1921) at the Aeolian Hall,

London. This champagnelike composition, based on a set of poems by Edith Sitwell, is performed by a speaker and small chamber ensemble playing sparklingly frivolous music, in a cheeky work typical of the naughty twenties. Apparently the title, *Façade* was inspired by a critical remark made on Edith Sitwell's poetry: "Very clever, no doubt, but what is she but a façade?" The poems are an emphatically rhythmical and seminonsensical tour de force, backed by music that corresponds to works by Satie, Ravel, Auric, Milhaud, Poulenc, Stravinsky, and Schoenberg. Commentators point to Schoenberg's *Pierrot Lunaire* (1912) as a possible influence because of the similarity in using spoken voice and chamber ensemble. But here the similarity ends, as Schoenberg's work invites one not into a world of frivolity, but into one of expressionist nightmare. In any case humour was lacking from Schoenberg's manically intense world; even when he tried to write in a humorous vein, as in the "comic" opera *Von Heute auf Morgen*, he did not succeed; Walton, on the other hand, was blessed with a good sense of humour. Thus the idea of using ensemble and spoken voice may be from Schoenberg, but the spirit of the work is far more akin to Satie's *Parade* (1917) and Stravinsky's *The Soldier's Tale* (1918). In spite of the fact, as Edith Sitwell's autobiography says, that the audience was hostile at the first performance, *Façade* has since then remained one of Walton's most popular compositions—so much so that he not only revised it several times, but also made two suites for orchestra based on its music: Suite No. 1 (1926) and Suite No. 2 (1938). Frederick Ashton also choreographed a ballet version.

A short flirtation with jazz followed, but was soon dropped with "disgust." *Siesta* for chamber orchestra, written in 1926, is still in a Mediterranean holiday mood and vaguely related to *Façade*, but the neoclassical style slowly creeps in with *Portsmouth Point* (1925), which looks back to the dance music of the past, and is most definitely apparent in the *Sinfonia Concertante* for piano and orchestra (1926–27), which was originally intended to be a ballet for Diaghilev.

The *enfant terrible* period was now over, and a more restrained romantic neoclassicism, inspired by Hindemith, Prokofiev, and Stravinsky, began to shape Walton's compositional thinking. In addition, entirely unexpectedly, an Elgarian lyrical nostalgia came to the surface, which eventually became the hallmark of Walton's musical style. This is clearly manifested in the Viola Concerto (1928–29), the idea for which was initiated by Sir Thomas Beecham, who had Lionel Tertis in mind as the soloist. When completed, the composer sent it to Tertis, who refused to play it, but Paul Hindemith, a viola player as well as a composer, agreed to give its first performance at a Promenade Concert in 1929. The lyrical theme in A minor, written in $\frac{9}{8}$ compound meter, is introduced by the solo viola. Its broad melodic outline confronts the listener with another major musical influence that molded Walton's thinking into that of the conservative-modern romantic lyricist he became: that is the profound influence of the music of Sibelius. The three movements unfold with masterly conviction, and the work as a whole is deservedly regarded as one of the great concertos of this century. As there are few compositions written for viola, it is likely to remain for a long time an unchallenged major work in the repertoire of viola players.

With his next major work, *Belshazzar's Feast* (1930–31), written for the Leeds Festival in 1931, Walton turned to the great favorite of the English choral tradition, oratorio, although he did not name it as such. Like Handel, who for dramatic reasons largely preferred subjects from the Old Testament, Walton and his librettist Osbert Sitwell turned to one of the most striking subjects in the Old Testament—the fall of Babylon, to which they added parts from Psalms 81 and 137 and Revelation. The work is conceived on a large scale, involving a baritone soloist, chorus, orchestra, and two brass bands. The overall effect, representing a pagan world, is harsh and stunning. Nothing of comparable impact in choral music had been written in England since Elgar's *Dream of Gerontius* and, on a smaller scale, Holst's *Hymn of Jesus*. Since its first performance, it has retained its place as one of the great choral masterpieces written by an English twentieth-century composer.

The honor of conducting the first performance of *Belshazzar's Feast* was Sir Malcolm Sargent's, but it was Sir Hamilton Harty who had the chance to conduct Walton's next major composition, his Symphony No. 1 (1932–35). Many believe it to be his finest work. It is certainly one of his most inventive compositions, especially the first movement. From the opening bars the soundworld of Sibelius—to whom the symphony is dedicated—is made self-evident, although transplanted into an English milieu. It is a well-documented fact that Sibelius had a major role in contributing to the developing of English symphonic writing. Several eminent composers—Bax, Vaughan Williams, and Walton—have not only dedicated compositions to Sibelius (for examples, Bax's Symphony No. 5 and Vaughan Williams's Symphony No. 5), thus acknowledging the great Finnish master, but they have also adopted certain procedures from him.

Walton's Symphony No. 1 is one of the most striking examples of how far Sibelius affected his symphonic thinking. Indeed, the popularity of Sibelius during the late 1920s and 1930s reached such a height that the shrewd critic Nevil Cardus commented in connection with Walton' Symphony No. 1: "It has been pretty certain for some time that if Sibelius did not hurry up and write his eighth symphony, somebody else would write it for him."[1] In general terms it could perhaps be argued that—regardless of one's own admiration of the works of Sibelius—his influence was less than beneficial for English music, as it slowed down modern developments by holding to the late-late romantic style, which was mistakenly acclaimed as modern. Sibelius, like Elgar, came at a historically significant moment. Each of them filled the musical vacuum into which they were born with a style characterized by late romantic nationalism based on Austro-German models. But by temperament, Sibelius had nothing to do with the twentieth century. His seven great symphonies—the last completed in 1924—are a late romantic expression, based on the dramatic tonal juxtaposition of the sonata principle and the Beethovian "conflict-triumph" aesthetic and moral principle. The partisanship of Cecil Gray and others in promoting Sibelius as the leading modern symphonist is understandable but misleading.

Much later, in 1960, Walton presented his Symphony No. 2 (1959–60). In comparison with the Symphony No. 1, it is on a more modest scale, but it is written in the typical masterly Waltonian style, and with much less evidence of Sibelius—although it might justifiably be queried whether the passacaglia Finale is a neoclassical influence, as the fugue was in the Symphony No. 1, or a gesture of musical solidarity with Brahms's Symphony No. 4.

Walton was a painstakingly meticulous, slow worker, who nevertheless composed—and successfully so—in most musical forms. In addition to the works already discussed he has left as his musical legacy his Violin Concerto (1938–39), a Cello Concerto (1956), two operas, *Troilus and Cressida* (1950–54) and *The Bear* (1965–67), and a distinguished selection of film music—for the film versions of several of Shakespere's plays and for the *First of the Few* (1942) and *The Battle of Britain* (1969). There is also a Violin Sonata, first performed by Yehudi Menuhin and Louis Kentner in 1950, a tribute to Hindemith in his *Variations on a Theme by Hindemith* (1962–63), and *Five Bagatelles* (1972) for guitar. Walton's works represent an impressive list of compositions, of which several have gained a secure position in the history of English music. Although he and his wife spent the largest part of their lives away from England in Italy, he became the "Grand Old Man" of British music in his Mediterranean stronghold, Ischia—a position that he held elegantly up to his death.

Constant Lambert (1905–51)

Lambert was born in London, but was of Australian origin. His father was a painter and his brother a sculptor. No wonder that, with such a background, his interest in the arts, including literature, was unusually wide-ranging. He studied at the Royal College of Music, where he was taught by, among others, Vaughan Williams. He, like Walton, was a friend of the Sitwells as well as of Cecil Gray, the music critic and composer, and of Walton, Warlock (see chapter 5, pp. 52–54), and others. He was a brilliant pianist and later an equally distinguished conductor, who, under the influence of French and Russian music, developed an early interest in ballet. In fact, his first crucial musical engagement came when, after being introduced to Diaghilev, he was promptly commissioned to write a ballet for the *Ballets Russes*. Lambert subsequently presented Diaghilev with his *Romeo and Juliet* (1924–25). Its first performance was given in 1926 at Monte Carlo. His idea was to have two tableaux in a form of a "rehearsal without scenery," and the decor was to be painted by his friend Christopher Wood. Instead, Diaghilev insisted on having surrealist decorations by Ernst and Miro. Despite the inevitable quarrel, *Romeo and Juliet* made a name for Lambert, not least because he was the first English composer to be commissioned by Diaghilev. His second ballet, *Pomana* (1926), was written for Nijinska. Neoclassical influence is apparent insofar as Lambert turned to seventeenth- and eighteenth-century dances for models. Both ballets are witty pastiches, but with a Lambertian bite to them.

His interest in music of the eighteenth century and of earlier periods stayed with him, as is manifested in his involvement with the music of William Boyce, some of whose music he edited, and his masque *Summer's Last Will and Testament* (1932–35), which is based on the poems of Thomas Nashe. French and Russian music, the ballet, neoclassicism and the music of the past were the basic ingredients of Lambert's evolving musical language, to which another, unmistakeable modern style of music—jazz—was added. All kinds of exoticism fascinated Lambert's imagination, including Chinese music, but jazz made a particularly marked impression on him. He admired Florence Mills, the jazz singer, and when she died he paid tribute by dedicating *Elegiac Blues* (1927) to her. Jazz style permeates his Piano Sonata (1928–29) and his most famous composition of all, the *Rio Grande* (1927), written to a poem of Sacheverell Sitwell, for piano, strings, brass, percussion, and chorus. This is a work that is "in the swing of things popular," not unlike the music of his great American contemporary, Gershwin. One of his last compositions was his blues- and jazz-inspired Concerto (1930–31) for piano and nine instruments.

Among his conducting activities, the most prestigious was his association with the Sadlers Wells Ballet from 1931 until 1947. As their musical director he greatly enhanced the reputation of the company. Moreover, he was also among the first leading participants of the BBC Third Programme, which started in 1946. His wide-ranging interests and involvements made him a considerable critic and staunch defender of things he liked—the music of Purcell, Puccini, Sibelius, popular music, and the then unfashionable Liszt. He was one of the most versatile men of his period. It is significant that nowadays he is perhaps less remembered as a composer, conductor, and master of ballet and jazz, than as the author of a notorious book, *Music Ho!* (1934), in which he set out to discuss the state of affairs in modern music. The book was subtitled *A Study of Music in Decline*. It is a period piece of "decline-writing" with parallels to that of Spengler and Ortega y Gasset. However, with its wit and atmospheric relevance, it is an immensely entertaining, infuriatingly opinionated book, which forms an often enlightening companion to *The Long Weekend—A Social History of Great Britain 1918–1939* by Robert Graves and Alan Hodge (1940).

Modernism was indeed included in the making of comtemporary England, but in a somewhat conservatve way. Ravel supposedly once said to Vaughan Williams concerning English music and musicians, "You have too many Sirs." Maybe the process of making artists part of the establishment has its price. Ironically, of the four composers discussed in this chapter, the one who remained modern in the most consistent manner and who was the least stuffy was the bohemian, erratic Lambert, who dissipated his enormous talent—but what fun he must have been!

5

Major Minor Masters: Ivor Gurney, Peter Warlock, E. J. Moeran, Gerald Finzi

A simpler heart than mine
    Might have seen beauty clear
Where I could see no sign
    Of Thee, but only fear.
Strengthen me, make me to see
    Thy beauty always
In every happening here.
        —Ivor Gurney (*In The Trenches,* 1917)

It is a common feature in histories of the arts that a major development, marked by the advent of several leading figures, is paralleled by the emergence of lesser figures whose contribution, although more restricted, nevertheless adds significantly to the character of a period. It is a popular truism that the work of genius goes beyond the boundaries of his own experiences and surroundings by transforming the personal and the local to the realm of the universal. On the other hand, what could be called the localized talent voices ideas that are of substantial value, while being circumscribed. All the same, the contribution of localized talent has an illuminating relevance without which ones appreciation of a period—indeed, of a country's cultural life—would be all the poorer. The four composers selected to be discussed in this chapter were men of talent whose works have enriched the musical and artistic life of England, although their output does not match in range or in quantity the leading composers' achievements. Three of them have in common that they wrote largely for voice—principally songs. English songwriting in this century is not only remarkably rich, being both abundant and distinguished, but also possesses a peculiarly English quality that is well worth any music lover's attention.

Ivor Gurney (1890–1937)

Gurney was a poet as well as a composer, and his composing focused appropriately on songwriting. He was born in Gloucester, the son of a tailor. After being a chorister at Gloucester Cathedral, he studied composition with Stanford at the Royal College of Music. He volunteered for military service at the outbreak of the First World War and served in the army until he was wounded and gassed in 1917. After treatment in army hospitals, he returned to the Royal College of Music, now studying with Vaughan Williams. During the years 1917 to 1920 he published two volumes of poetry: *Severn and Somme* (1917) and *War's Embers* (1919). His first music publication came in 1920 when a set of songs he had written some time earlier, *Five Elizabethan Songs*, was published. Gurney was very pleased with his *Five Elizabethan Songs*, and his style stressed their Englishness. The idea of using two flutes, two clarinets, two bassoons, and a harp for accompaniment demonstrates his inspired stylishness.

Gurney tried to find a suitable job, but was unsuccessful. How far this was a consequence of eccentric instability exacerbated by his war experience is difficult to assess. These tragic tendencies were, in any case, combined with a probably justified sense of feeling unwanted—the fate of many artists. After threatening suicide in letters sent to friends, he made several attempts, and he was admitted to a mental hospital in Gloucester and declared insane in 1922; he was later taken to the City of London Mental Hospital, where he stayed until his death in 1937. Although the bulk of his songs were composed during the years from 1919 to 1922, including two Housman song cycles *Ludlow and Teme* (1919) and *The Western Playland* (1919), and a set of six songs on the poems of Edward Thomas, *Lights Out* (1918–25), he continued to write and compose. Kind friends, such as Finzi, Howells, Marion Scott, and others, undertook the task of selecting and editing his work for publication and posterity. As a songwriter his ancestry is not so much based on the Austro-German model, the *Lied*, but on something more typical of the English tradition: the work of Renaissance courtier poets, such as Thomas Campion, who were also inspired musicians. James Reeves in his brilliant introduction to *Georgian Poetry* writes: "The faults of Georgian poetry at its most ordinary were technical slackness . . . ."[1] Gurney, as a composer, shared this weakness with his fellow Georgians. Lack of precision and reliance on too much of the instinctive and the impulsive made much of his writing unpolished. The totality of his output is relatively small, but the best of it, nevertheless, conjures up a better understanding of the nature of music and poetry, above all, of Georgian poetry, which he represented with such tragic individuality both as a musician and poet.

Peter Warlock (1894–1930)

Warlock, whose real name was Philip Heseltine, was a most colourful personality with something of the Hoffmannesque or Schumannesque in his mental makeup. His choice of two names for his two activities—Heseltine for his literary work, and Warlock for his musical activities—is not unlike Schumann's own assumption of a dual personality in the form of Florestan and Eusebius. The one, Eusebius/Heseltine, was the introvert, shy and sensitive. The other, Florestan/Warlock, was the extrovert, boisterous and daredevilish. (Warlock, of course, means "in league with the devil.") Like Gurney, Warlock is chiefly remembered for his songs and for his extraordinary personality. He, too, was forced to interrupt his studies because of the First World War, but was unfit for service; in any case he was a conscientious objector. He had no formal education in music apart from what he had picked up at Eton, where he was introduced to Delius, whom he much revered. Not only did they think highly of each other, but a lasting friendship also developed between the two, and Warlock eventually wrote a perceptive book about Delius. It was inevitable that his music should be influenced by that of Delius; added to which there was the later intellectual stimulus of Bernard van Dieren, a Dutch composer living in England. Dieren was one of many in the Sitwell's entourage who made something of a name for himself in the 1920s on grounds that today seem to have been based on rather generous wishful thinking within the clique. (In fact, his book on Epstein and a collection of criticism, *Down Among the Dead*, published shortly before his death, are more interesting than his music.)

Although Warlock kept a keen ear open to musical developments on the Continent, his deepest involvement was with the Elizabethan period, of which he was an acknowledged connoisseur, and with the music of Purcell. He was a dedicated editor of works from both the sixteenth and seventeenth centuries and wrote on topics such as Arbeau's *Orchesographie*, to which he contributed a preface (1925) written in collaboration with one of the most brilliant critics of the time, Cecil Gray. He also published Carlo Gesualdo: Musician and Murderer (1926) and a discourse entitled English Ayres, Elizabethan and Jacobean (1932). His critical talent and musicological inclination led him to launch two musical journals, *The Sackbut* and, later, the short-lived *Milo*.

So far as his personal life was concerned, his bohemian way of living upset his relations with both his friends and his family. His friendship with D. H. Lawrence ended in a quarrel; so did his marriage—the couple separated after seven years.

It has already been seen that, especially in the case of Bax, that Ireland held a fascination—it still does—and made a considerable impression on the imaginations of several artists well beyond its shores. The poets of the Celtic revival, headed by one of its leading poets, Yeats, were inspiring composers to set their works to music, and, indeed, from Yeats to Joyce, many Irish poets have been set to music by English composers. As if by fate, the Irish literary renaissance was paralleled by the English musical renaissance, and it had an intrinsic role to play in the development of English music. Celtic exoticism has an emotional pull over and above the pull of "foreign" exoticism such as, say, the Russian or Mediterranean, by virtue of its closer cultural ties; its thrills are more accessible. It is not surprising, therefore, to find that Warlock's most precious song setting is based on his own selection of four poems by Yeats. *The Curlew* (1920–22), written for tenor, flute, English horn, and string quartet, alone would ensure that Warlock is remembered even if he had never written anything else. The sustained sadness of the poems is matched by Warlock's empathetic musical settings. Its desolation has few parallels in the history of

European music, and in English music it has no peer. The fact that Schubert's *Winterreise* and some of the songs from *Schwanengesang* come to mind in the context of this work is a measure of Warlock's standing as a songwriter.

He wrote very little for the orchestra, but his delightful neoclassical composition the *Capriol Suite* (1926), consisting of six arrangements of old French dances from Arbeau's *Orchesographie*, is one that is likely to stay in the repertoire. The persona of Warlock proved too much, however, for Heseltine. One day, after putting the cat outside the door, he killed himself.

Edward James Moeran (1894–1950)

Whereas for Bax and Warlock Celtic culture was a deeply felt but imported intellectual and emotional relationship, for Moeran it was a real inheritance, as his ancestors were Irish. Like Bax and Warlock, he too paid visits to Ireland. Moreover, he married an Irish woman and died in Kenmore, Ireland. But equally powerful were his roots in Norfolk, where his father was a clergyman. Educated at a public school and at the Royal College of Music, his studies, like those of Gurney and Warlock, were interrupted by the Great War. A severe head wound put him out of action in 1917. Returning from service he was appointed music master at his old school. Further studies followed with John Ireland.

During the 1920s Moeran slowly emerged as a composer of distinction. The vogue for rhapsodic writing in the period is reflected in his first two orchestral Rhapsodies, no. 1 (1922) and no. 2 (1924), together with the later Rhapsody (1943) for piano and orchestra. His music shows the strong influence of Delius and of his teacher, Ireland. But his preoccupation with the folk songs of Norfolk and Suffolk—he himself was a folk song collector—gives his music a characteristic lyricism and pastoral smoothness that is based on diatonic and modal harmonic orientation and that is apparent in his *Six Norfolk Folk-Songs* (first performed in 1923) and *Six Suffolk Folk-Songs* (first performed in 1931).

The romantic love of nature that permeates his music, giving it a mysterious, rustic quality, places him among those of his contemporaries, above all Vaughan Williams, whose music reflects, in a most distinctive manner, the Englishness of English music. Nowhere is this more so than in one of the greatest of his compositions, the Symphony in G minor (1934–37). Characteristically, Moeran provided the information that the symphony was conceived "among the mountains and seaboard of County Kerry" as well as "around the sanddunes and marches of East Norfolk." The lyrical, folk song-like themes are held together by a symphonic thinking inspired by Sibelius, but there is a major difference between Siebelius's symphonic thinking and Moeran's. Moeran's strength lies in the expression of gently lyrical, pastoral mood; his weakness is a lack of real drama, real conflict. In Sibelius's finales, the music surges towards an apotheosis of moral triumph expressed by purely musical means—that is, by an overwhelming, nobly vindicatory tune. In comparison, Moeran's Finale is labored, the dramatic struggle and the sense of abyss was entirely alien from his soul.

The writing of a symphony was a turning point in his reluctant relationship with the orchestra, as it was followed by a Violin Concerto (1942), then by a brilliant *Sinfonietta* (1944) and the *Irish Cello Concerto* (1945) for Peers Coetmore, his wife-to-be.

His friendship with Warlock, with whom he lived for a while had a beneficial impact on his composition, especially his songs. Moeran, too, was drawn to Irish poetry and set some of Joyce's poems in *Chamber Music,* under the title *Seven Poems of James Joyce* (1929). Stephen Banfield, in his outstanding study *Sensibility and English Song* (1985), sums up the profound Irishness inherent in Moeran's music:

> Although an Irish jig can be sensed as early as "The Lads in their Hundreds" from his Housman cycle of 1920, the Joyce songs are the first work in which he overtly responds to Irish folk melody, on which he drew in his music more than did Warlock, Hadley or Bax.[2]

Moeran, too, has added his name, with his song cycle *Ludlow Town* (1920), to the distinguished list of composers who have made settings of Housman's poems. *A Shropshire Lad* became the symbol of a whole period. Its author, the strange professor of Latin at Cambridge and translator of risqué Latin authors, who became the "spiritual father of the Georgian movement"—which in essence was a nostalgic "celebration of rural England"—little knew that he would make such an impact on musicians and that his name would be linked with one of the most glorious chapters in the history of English music. As for Morean, he has a minor place among the giants, but whenever his music is played it continues to contribute to the "celebrations of England."

Gerald Finzi (1901–56)

Although born in London, or perhaps because of it, Finzi longed for the tranquillity of the countryside. Thus during his life, he moved to Gloucestershire, then to Wiltshire, and after that to Hampshire, where he built a house and started growing apples. A man of independent means, he lived for the pursuit of beauty, cultivating his own sensibility and fine understanding of music and poetry. His basically retiring, inward-looking nature appears in his largely vocal compositions, which are at their best when they echo his gently contemplative nature.

His orchestral compositions are hardly ever featured nowadays in the concert repertoire, although his Violin Concerto (1928) was conducted by Vaughan Williams, who, together with Elgar, deeply influenced him. Finzi also wrote a Clarinet Concerto (op. 31, 1948–49) and a Cello Concerto (op. 40, 1951–55), among other miscellaneous compositions. However, the choice of concerto form by a basically nondramatic composer was ill-advised. These works, as well as others, are let down by a pastoral, undramatic mood, that fails to grip—a feature of Finzi's music that he shares with Moeran.

Finzi's claim for a place in the history of British music largely rest on *Dies natalis,* op. 8 (1926–39) and his fine settings of several of Hardy's poems. *Dies natalis* (which means birthday in Latin) is a cantata for solo voice (either soprano or tenor) and string ensemble. It has five movements, of which four (nos. 2–5) are settings of a prose passage and three poems of Traherne, a seventeenth-century clergyman who, influenced by Neoplantonic thought, wrote ecstatic poems and prose and who, in his *Centuries of Meditation,* described his childhood in a strikingly evocative manner. This topic touched a common chord in Finzi who had something of a fixation on his childhood: his father died when he was eight and he lost three of his brothers in those years. Using the model of the greatest of all predecessors in cantata writing—Bach—he succeeded in creating a noble musical setting of contemplative character, which, regarded in terms of a stylistic cocktail, would be a mixture of Bach, Parry, Elgar, Gurney, Fauré, Vaughan Williams—all adding up to an authentic Finzi.

His setting of Hardy's poems—*A Young Man's Exhortation*, op. 14 (1933), *Earth and Air and Rain* (1936), *Before and After Summer*, op. 16 (1949), *I Said to Love* (1958), *Till Earth Outwears* (1958)—are among his best songs, in spite of the fact that superficially there was but very little similarity between poet and composer. Yet the intellect and, above all, the emotions have their own ways. Finzi fully understood Hardy's world of struggle and suffering and the principle of "the implanted crookedness of things," as R. L. Binyon put it. (Binyon's drama, *Arthur* [1923], was enriched by Elgar's incidental music.) There lurked behind the cheerful and kindly social countenance of Finzi a fatalistic sense of the abyss. In his orchestral works he had no strength to give expression to this, but he was the master in his songs. He was also able to put into words his *ars poetica* in his preface to *Abraham's Place: Catalogue of Works* (1941, 1951), quoted by Stephen Banfield in his book *Sensibility and English Song:*

It was Thomas Hardy who wrote "Why do I go on doing these things?" . . . some curious force compels us to preserve and project into the future the essence of our individuality, and, in doing so, to project something of our age and civilisation. The artist is like the coral insect, building his reef out of the transitory world around him and making a solid structure to last long after his own fragile and uncertain life. It is one of the many proud points of his occupation that, great or small, there is, ultimately, little else but his work through which his coming and civilisation may be known and judged by posterity. . . . Something is created out of nothing, order out of chaos; and as we succeed in shaping our intractable material into coherence and form, a relief comes to the mind (akin to the relief experienced at the remembrance of some forgotten thing) as a new accretion is added to that projection of oneself which, in metaphor, has been called "Absolam's place" or a coral reef or a "ceder or schrubbe" . . . . As usually happens, it is likely that new ideas, new fashions, and the pressing forward of new generations, will soon obliterate my small contribution. Yet I like to think that in each generation may be found a few responsive minds, and for them I should still like my work to be available. To shake hands with a good friend over the centuries is a pleasant thing, and the affection which an individual may retain after his departure is perhaps the only thing which guarantees an ultimate life to his works.[3]

Finzi can rest assured there will be a "few responsive minds" and a few "good friends" with whom he can shake hands.

The British musical scene of the first half of this century could be described as a period of British idealism, an idealism characterised by a strongly upheld belief in humanistic values and a love of the countryside. The composers in this and earlier chapters were seekers of beauty who did their utmost, in spite of everything, to "look up to the heavenly stars."

6

A Genius with a Common Touch:
Benjamin Britten

Peace is not silent, it is the voice of love
—From the libretto of *Owen Wingrave*

It is of symbolic significance that one of the greatest of English composers in this century, Benjamin Britten (1913–76), happened to be born on 22 November, the feast day of St. Cecilia, the patron saint of music. He came from a music-loving family in which his mother seems to have dominated the scene culturally—above all in things musical—as she played the piano and also liked singing. Regular musical evenings with performing guest musicians were part of the family life in which the young Britten matured. The formative impact of such congenial activities must have helped to develop his musical interests at a very early age. Indeed he started composing at the prodigiously early age of five. His progress was rapid, and, by the age of nine, he was playing duets and accompanying his mother's singing, as well as learning to play the viola.

Until the age of eleven he was largely self-taught in composition, but when Frank Bridge came to East Anglia, Britten became his pupil. From him he learned the craft of composition and what it meant to be a professional musician. His experience of school music, or rather the lack of it, followed by his not too happy three years at the Royal College of Music (1930–33), where he studied composition with Ireland, made him realise the low status music had in Britain and how oppressive militant officials of parochialism could be. The following anecdote illustrates his experiences: when he was given a traveling scholarship, the Royal College of Music authorities managed to bar him from going to Vienna where he had hoped to study with Alban Berg. They viewed the continental avant-garde with something akin to moral revulsion.

Having first largely been influenced by Austro-German music, Britten now turned this attention to other models: the music of Purcell and the composes of the English Madrigal School. His first published composition appeared during his student days at the Royal College of Music. The *Sinfonietta*, op. 1 (1932), for chamber orchestra is a brilliant work written by a young composer intent on displaying his talents but nevertheless keeping within the boundaries of good taste. Already Britten was showing a classical restraint and acute aural sophistication and clarity. His preoccupation with the variation form was a characteristic feature of his compositions, as Scott Goddard has pointed out in *British Music of Our Time*.[1] Britten's next published work, *A Boy Was Born*, op. 3, for unaccompanied chorus, was written during the years 1932 to 1933. It is a set of variations—a highly original form for chorus—demonstrating great musical imagination and brilliance in its writing, although in its first version the voices were stretched a little.

Not unlike Walton, Britten also made an early entrée in the artistic world of the day. One of the most outstanding figures whom he befriended was W. H. Auden. Britten was now living the life of a professional composer in London, taking any commission he could. He agreed to write film music for the GPO Film Unit where the artistic director was John Grieson. Britten was to contribute music to several semidocumentary film fantasies, most notably to *Coal Face* and *Night Mail* (both 1936). His first meeting with Auden came about through the GPO Film Unit, for which Auden wrote the scripts. Collaboration on the documentaries was followoed by their working on a symphonic song cycle, *Our Hunting Fathers*, op. 8 (1936), for solo voice and orchestra, which was performed at the Norwich Festival. Technical brilliance founded on an inspired aural imagination and preoccupation with the variation form were so far the characteristic attributes of the young Britten. To these another lasting interest should be added: his involvement in writing for children. A didactic humanism became a discreet yet deeply felt attitude of his. An early example of this is his setting of children's songs with piano accompaniment, *Friday Afternoons*, op. 7 (1933–35). This was written for a boys' school where his brother was headmaster. The twelve songs show Britten's uncanny ability to say a lot with the simplest of means, an attribute that stayed with him the rest of his life.

His delightful *Soirées musicales,* op. 9 (1936), an arrangement of Rossini's music, was followed by one of his first major orchestral compositions, *Variations on a Theme of Frank Bridge, op. 10 (1937).* The theme was taken from his respected teacher's *Idyll* No. 2 for string quartet. It received its first performance at the Salzburg Festival.

Like so many of his contemporaries, Britten was deeply affected by the Spanish Civil War. Indeed, just before its outbreak, he visited Barcelona in order to take part in the festival organized by the International Society for Contemporary Music Festival. There he met Lennox Berkeley, and the two of them not only collected some Catalan dances, but also collaborated in writing an orchestral suite based on them. The Catalan title given to this suite was *Mont Juic* (op. 12, 1936–37), a famous hill on the outskirts of Barcelona. The *Ballad of Heroes,* op. 14 (1939), to poems of W. H. Auden and R. Swingler was written in memory of those British men who died in the Spanish Civil War.

In 1939 Britten, like so many others of his contemporaries, felt, if not disillusioned, at least restless about the state of affairs surrounding him. Auden and Isherwood left for America, and soon both Britten and Peter Pears, his lifelong companion, decided to follow suit and left for New York. They went in the hope of a brighter future, and certainly, for a while, America proved stimulating. There Britten composed his Violin Concerto, op. 15 (1939), and *Diversions,* op. 21 (1940), a work for piano written for the left hand of Paul Wittgenstein who had lost his right arm in the First Wold War. At this time there were also the two magnificent song cycles *Les illuminations,* op. 18 (1939), on the prose-poems of Rimbaud, and the *Seven Sonnets of Michelangelo,* op. 22 (1940). Among other works written in America were two unaccompanied choral compositions, one on a text by Auden, *Hymn to St. Cecilia,* op. 27 (1942), and the other, the inspired *A Ceremony of Carols,* op. 28 (1942), for high voices and harp. Britten seriously contemplated taking up American citizenship, but homesickness combined with a sense of solidarity made him conclude otherwise. A chance reading of an article by E. M. Forster on the Suffolk poet

George Crabbe in which Forster emphatically stressed Crabbe's Englishness, touched a sympathetic chord in Britten's mind. He bought a copy of Crabbe's poems and read *The Borough*, which gave him the first idea for his operatic masterpiece *Peter Grimes*, op. 33.

The three years that Britten spent in America made him realize where his roots were. The uprooted state of an emigré did not suit him; he did not share Stravinsky's cosmopolitan savoir faire; he needed his national roots. Britten and Pears decided to return to England, and they did so in 1942 on the condition that they should be able to give recitals. This arrangement enabled Britten to remain a pacifist and be exempt from military service while still serving the nation artistically during the Second World War.

During the remainder of the war, Britten wrote the *Serenade*, op. 31 (1943), for tenor, French horn, and strings, based on a selection of texts ranging from a fifteenth-century dirge, to Blake, Cotton, Jonson, Keats, and Tennyson. Significantly, he also started a series of folk song arrangements that appeared between 1945 and 1948 in three volumes: *Volume I: British, Volume II: French,* and *Volume III: British.* But the most famous work of the years 1944 to 1945 was his opera *Peter Grimes* (1945), inspired by Crabbe's poem. It received his first performance, with Pears in the title role, a month after the ending of the war in 1945. It was an instant success and a milestone in the history of English music. The tragic figure of the fisherman of Aldeburgh became subject of symbolic proportions, not only in representing in verismo style man's struggle with nature, the sea, and community life, but also at a personal level in portraying, in a masterly fashion, the outcast who is stigmatized for being what he is—or perhaps for what he is not—according to common expectation. Like Alban Berg and Janáček, Britten elevated the parochial to something of universal interest. As he himself said:

> For most of my life I have lived closely in touch with the sea. My parents' house in Lowestoft directly faced the sea, and my life as a child was coloured by the fierce storms that sometimes drove ships onto our coast and ate away whole stretches of the neighbouring cliffs. In writing Peter Grimes, I wanted to express my awareness of the perpetual struggle of man and woman whose livelihood depends on the sea. . . .[2]

Britten's attraction to the music of Purcell took the form of a self-conscious cultivation of the last great English master before Elgar. He shared Purcell's interest in the variation form, above all the passacaglia and ground bass style, as well as operatic composition. This seeking out of Purcell was a symbolic gesture, a picking up of the broken historical thread as it were. No wonder that several of his compositions not only show the influence of Purcell, but were dedicated to him as an act of homage. The two hundred and fiftieth anniversary of the death of Purcell was in 1945, and the nine *Holy Sonnets of John Donne,* op. 35 (1945), for tenor and piano, in which the defeat of death is celebrated (composed after visiting German concentration camps) and the String Quartet No. 2, op. 36 (1945), with its passacaglia Finale, were written in order to celebrate the occasion. One of Britten's stunning orchestral compositions, written for an educational film, *The Instruments of the Orchestra,* and generally known as the *Young Person's Guide to the Orchestra,* op. 34 (1946), is based on a theme of Purcell's. Britten's idea was to illustrate, in the form of a set of variations, the nature of instruments and their orchestral sections, leading to a fugue that brings all the instruments into a glorious finale. He succeeded in bringing Purcell's theme, from his incidental music to the play *Abdelazer,* to an apotheosis in which Purcell's theme is combined with the theme of the fugue. Few orchestral compositions give such an elevating experience. The fact that Janáček's *Sinfonietta* (1926), Bartók's *Concerto for Orchestra* (1942–43), and Kodály's *Peacock Variations* (1938–39) come to mind in the context of this work is a reflection of Britten's genius. The didactic background should not mislead the listener—the *Variations and Fugue on a Theme by Purcell,* as the piece is subtitled, is one of the orchestral masterpieces of British music.

Britten was frequently referred to as "an heir of Purcell," and he emerged not only as a major composer, but as a composer of operatic genius. Encouraged by the success of *Peter Grimes,* Britten turned to another operatic subject, which was suggested to him by Eric Crozier, culminating in *The Rape of Lucretia,* op. 37 (1946), to a libretto by Ronald Duncan. In contrast to the large scale of *Peter Grimes, Lucretia* is a chamber opera in size, calling for only eight singers and a small orchestra. In many ways *Lucretia* is a neoclassical work, that is, a revival of the Baroque operatic style in the middle of twentieth-century England, and, as such, it owes something to Stravinsky's *Oedipus Rex* (1926–27), which Britten admired. As opposed to *Peter Grimes*, which is quasi-realistic and near contemporary, *Lucretia* is based on a classical story of ancient Rome. However, the violation of Lucretia, followed by her death, stresses a characteristic preoccupation of Britten with innocence and its loss in a cruel world where the individual finds himself helpless. In their own ways, both Peter Grimes and Lucretia are helpless victims of circumstance. Lucretia's funeral march is based on a chaconne, yet again illustrating one of Britten's compositional insignias. Incidentally, the title role was first sung by the then unknown Kathleen Ferrier.

Britten was now searching for a suitable subject for a comic opera. The result was *Albert Herring*, op. 39 (1947). The libretto is an adaption of a Maupassant story, *Le Rosier de Mme. Husson.* The transference of the original tale to a small market town in East Suffolk is a strange choice—it is perhaps better not to know the French original. The humor is on occasion heavy going, tending towards caricature. Like *Lucretia, Albert Herring* is scored for a chamber ensemble with twenty-four performers in all. Albert Herring is a "mummy's boy," who is chosen to be May King because of his chaste life and because there are no suitable girls in town to be elected as May Queen. Herring's shy and subordinate way of life, however, changes, to everybody's surprise or delight; he becomes something of a rampaging libertine, thus freeing himself from his previously oppressed existence. Again, Britten's preoccupation with lost innocence is demonstrated, but in this case it does not lead to tragedy; on the contrary, the tone is positive, since losing one's innocence is viewed as part of life, a process towards maturity. The French film version of the story with Fernandel is more humorous, but Britten's music has brilliant moments with its diatonic world of innocent fun. Its first performance, like that of *Lucretia,* was given in Glyndebourne, with scenery and costumes designed by John Piper and with Britten conducting.

In 1947 Britten and Pears decided to run their own festival, and for this purpose moved to 4 Crabbe Street, Aldeburgh. The first Aldeburgh Festival in 1948 gave the first performance of his cantata *St. Nicholas,* op. 42, depicting the life and death of the fourteenth-century saint and based on a text by Eric Crozier. Crozier was also the librettist for his children's opera *Let's Make An Opera,* op. 45 (1949)—an "Entertainment for young people." The work is ingeniously divided into two parts: in the first part both children and adults are in the process of making an opera; in the second part they are actually performing the result of their labor. The audience is called on to participate actively in four songs. It is a delightfully didactic work, involving everyone present.

Since its first festival, Aldeburgh has established itself as a major festival town that has given first performances not only of several of Britten's compositions, but of other contemporary composers as well. Moreover, the organizers have also had a policy of reviving works by neglected musicians.

In 1949 Britten completed his choral symphony, the *Spring Symphony,* op. 44, which takes the overall pattern of a four-movement symphony in which there are fourteen poems about spring scored for soloists, orchestra, and chorus. The range of the selection of poets makes a virtual anthology of English poems about spring. It comprises Spenser, Nashe, Milton, and Blake among others, and includes W. H. Auden's fine *Out on the lawn I lie my bed.* For a precursor, Holst's *Choral Symphony* comes to mind, but even more crucial was Britten's affinity with the music of Mahler, which exercised a great influence on his musical thinking. This influence he shared with his Russian contemporary Shostakovich who, by the way dedicated to Britten his Symphony No. 14 in which eleven poems, written by modern poets such as Apollinaire and Lorca, are included. The idea of blending symphonic structure with the *Lied,* so dear to Mahler, was taken up by both Britten and Shostakovich, who also shared the view that in certain compositions it was important to put across a message. The abstract classical symphonic thinking was gradually augmented by words in order to make sure that the messages were understood. This humanistic concept, which goes back at least as far as Beethoven's Symphony No. 9, serves as an aid towards understanding. *Billy Budd,* op. 50 (1951), was Britten's next major operatic venture, for which his choice was the American novelist Herman Melville's story, shaped into a libretto by E. M. Forster and Eric Crozier. It is an all-male counterpart of *Peter Grimes,* where the sea again dominates the scene: the whole opera takes place on board HMS *Indomitable* at the end of the eighteenth century.

Billy Budd is a fine and courageous piece of operatic composition with some vintage Britten in its melodic and orchestral writing. Yet, whereas in *Peter Grimes* the outcast, the outsider, is allegorical—and indeed the insinuated guilt of Grimes is metamorphosed into a universally shareable human experience—*Billy Budd,* with its all-male cast gravitating towards homosexual attraction, gives a lopsided impression that not even Britten's genius could balance. One could, of course, argue that there is no need for balance and that sexual deviations—sadism and so on—are also part of the human condition and have therefore a legitimate place in any artistic expression—a subject is to be judged on its own merit. Nevertheless, in spite of its unquestionable musical distinction and the fact that it has slowly become a well-established operatic work frequently performed—at any rate in England—it has remained a perplexing operatic essay. The rather unfortunate coincidence that during the gestation period of *Billy Budd,* Britten revised and performed Gay's *Beggar's Opera,* op. 43 (1948), gave the local wits an opportunity to poke fun at the expense of the composer by calling *Billy Budd* "The Bugger's Opera." Be that as it may, *Billy Budd* is one of Britten's most densely written compositions that has, if anything, been improved since the original four-act version was revised to two (1960). Once more, Britten and his librettists were concerned with the clashing forces of good and evil and with the Wagnerian redemption concept. The climax of the opera, at which point Vere is redeemed through the love of the Christ-like figure Billy, is a musico-dramatic experience that should not be missed.

Imogen Holst, daughter of Gustav Holst, became Britten's assistant in 1952. They had already worked together in 1951 on a new realization of Purcell's *Dido and Aeneas.* The coronation of Queen Elizabeth II was celebrated with his next opera, named *Gloriana,* op. 53 (1953), after Elizabeth I. The libretto was written by William Plomer, the South African poet and novelist, who based it on Lytton Strachey's *Elizabeth and Essex,* a rather erotic and post-Freudian piece of historical writing. It was an understandable yet curious choice of subject. Nevertheless, the mottolike theme, written in Bulgarian rhythm and sung by the chorus (crowd) in act 1 in praise of the Queen, is relevant enough:

> Green leaves are we, Red Rose our Golden Queen,
> O crowned rose among the leaves so green.

It has not proved to be Britten's best-loved composition. Nevertheless, he was created Companion of Honour on 1 June 1953, a week before the first performance of *Gloriana* at Covent Garden in the presence of Queen Elizabeth II.

As so often with Britten, and indeed with many great artists, he had hardly finsihed one work before his mind was already on another subject, or indeed, subjects. The song cycle of eight poems, for which he used the title of Hardy's last volume of poetry, *Winter Words* (op. 52, 1953), was immediately followed by the composition of what is arguably one of his most striking operas, and for many his best: *The Turn of the Screw*, op. 54 (1954). Based on an adaption of a Henry James short story, the writing of the libretto fell to John Piper's wife, Myfanwy, who suggested the idea to Britten in the first place. The story, with its strongly psychological and sexual undertones, is as follows: at the start a young governess who is the narrator is introduced. She is on her way to Bly in order to look after two orphaned children, Miles and Flora, who are both blessed by beauty and charm. The head of the household is their uncle, a good-looking man, towards whom the new governess is strangely attracted. All seems well, but soon she senses the powerful presence of evil in the form of two ghostly apparitions: Peter Quint, the libertine ex-valet, and Miss Jessel, the ex-governess, who had an apparently sinful relationship when they were living in the house. The new governess becomes obsessed with the idea that the children are under their evil influence, and she decides to save them. In a nightmarish scene, Flora is saved and taken to safety by the housekeeper Mrs. Grose, but the little boy dies in the governess's arms while she fights against the evil Peter Quint.

The listeners are left to decide for themselves whether these apparitions are the governess's own fantasies, based on suppressed sexual desire that she feels for the handsome uncle, further fired by the stories of Mrs. Grose, and that she tries to exorcise, or whether there is indeed evil in the memory of the two lovers that, in a cancerous way, eats into the souls of the living well after the events and manages to involve even the children, finally claiming the life of one of them. Ultimately the viewer is left guessing, for as Henry James himself stated, the story is "a trap for the unwary."

The structure of the music is quite unusual (even if one takes into account Berg's *Wozzeck* [1917–22]), as it is designed to be a chamber opera in two acts based on a theme and fifteen variations. The theme is based on a nonserial twelve-tone row. The sustained intensity of it is superb. Britten, as always, uses special sound effects, like bells, a brief piano-concerto-like scene within the opera, the symbolic use of keys, including the black-notes being overcome by the triumphant white-notes, and so on. It is certainly as much of a masterpiece as *Peter Grimes,* and perhaps even more so.

Britten's only ballet, *The Prince of the Pagodas,* op. 57 (1957), was inspired by a visit to the Far East. The impact of this visit is reflected in the Oriental orchestral effects that he introduced in his score.

With *Noye's Fludde,* op. 59 (1957), Britten turned again to didactic composition with audience participation. Based on the setting of the *Chester Miracle Play* (miracle or biblical dramas were popular in England from the Middle Ages until the Renaissance), it calls for amateurs and professionals alike, as well as children, who are dressed up as animals and birds to be saved by Noye. There are three hymns to be sung by all, including the congregationlike audience. It is a sheer delight and a diatonic bliss of regained innocence for all.

The *Missa brevis,* op. 63 (1959), for boy's voices and organ, dedicated to George Malcolm and the choir of Westminster Cathedral, belongs, like its precursor *A Ceremony of Carols,* to the genre of Britten's humanistic worship through art and tradition. It represents a profound vindication of values.

A Midsummer Night's Dream, op. 64 (1960), is an opera based on an adaption of Shakespeare's play by Britten and Pears, and it succeeds in retaining much of the charm and poetry of the original. The libretto concentrates on the fairies and above all on Oberon. In addition, most of it is set in the wood, thus emphasizing the fairy side of Shakespeare's play. Casting the boys as fairies and making Oberon a countertenor is one of those many masterly strokes of originality with which Britten surprised his audiences in the course of four decades. The three main groups of protagonists, the fairies, lovers, and craftsmen, are musically emphasized in a most ingenious way. The orchestral effects are brilliant, but in spite of such unforgettable moments as the closing section of act 3 in which Oberon, Titania, and the Fairies are singing:

> Now until the break of day,
> Through this house each Fairy stray

the overall impression is that the work is somewhat lacking in the warmth and sustained playful magic of Mendelssohn's incidental music for the same play. This is perhaps an unfair and even futile comparison, yet it is one that is bound to be made by some listeners.

To celebrate the opening of the resurrected Coventry Cathedral, which was blitzed into ruins during the last war, Britten was commissioned to write a sacred work, and the result was the *War Requiem,* op. 60 (1962). If there was any question about who was the greatest English composer of the time, this work gave a definite answer. It is not only a towering religious masterpiece by a modern English composer, but one of the most significant sacred compositions of this century.

Characteristically, Britten chose to blend the traditional Latin text of the requiem with the unforgettable war poems of Wilfred Owen, who died at the very end of the First World War. The rest is an overwhelming expression, in both sacred and secular terms, of sympathy with man's suffering and the tagic waste of war. The score is dedicated to four of Britten's friends, all killed in the Second World War, to which he added a quotation from Owen:

> My subject is War, and the pity of War.
> The Poetry is in the pity.
> All a poet can do today is warn.

After finishing *A Midsummer Night's Dream* and at about the time immediately after the composition of the majestic *War Requiem,* Britten was mainly occupied in writing works for his friend Mstislav Rostropovich: the Cello Sonata, op. 65 (1961), and Cello Symphony, op. 68 (1963), and also the three Cello Suites, opp. 72, 80, and 87 (1964, 1967, and 1971).

It was in the mid-1950s, when Britten was in Tokyo, that he had the opportunity of seeing for the first time performances of Noh plays. The solemn dignity of the performance, together with the tradition that actors, musicians, and chorus should appear on the same platform so as to achieve the maximum dramatic intensity, left a deep impression on him. The play that impressed him was the medieval Japanese Noh play *Sumidagawa* by Juno Motomasu, in which a mother, who has gone mad, is in search of her lost son. Britten saw a similarity between this play and medieval English sacred drama, a similarity that he believed could be fruitfully developed. In the composer's own words:

> Surely the Medieval Religious Drama in England would have made a comparable setting—an all male cast of ecclesiastics—a single austere staging in a church—a very limited instrumental accompaniment—a moral story? And so we came from *Sumidagawa* to *Curlew River* and a church in the Fens, but with the same story and similar characters and whereas in Tokyo the music was the ancient Japanese music jealously preserved by successive generations, here I have started the work with that wonderful plainsong hymn *"Te lucis ante terminum,"* and from it the whole piece may be said to have grown.[3]

Curlew River, op. 71 (1964), is thus not only a neomedieval church parable, but it also demonstrates, in a highly imaginative fashion, how fruitful the cross-fertilization of ideas can be between the Orient and the West.

Two more parables followed *Curlew River, The Burning Fiery Furnace,* op. 77 (1966), based on the Book of Daniel, and *The Prodigal Son,* op. 81 (1968), the last being based on one of the most popular biblical tales, which has inspired several artists in the past in the fields of fine art, literature, and music. All three librettos are by William Plomer. As so often before, in these three church parables, Britten again succeeded in evoking intense dramatic effects by the simplest of means. His prodigious sense of hearing unfailingly led him to sophisticated simplicity that few could parallel. When, for example, the Prodigal Son is in utter despair and bitterness and is lamenting his foolishness just before his decision to return home, he sings a chromatic passage echoed on the viola:

> With joy I sowed, my harvest is despair,
> The end is bitterness, this is the end.

This scene has a dramatic intensity that has its root not so much in modern chromatic writings, as in the Renaissance madrigal and lute song writings of the mannerists' style.

During the years 1965 and 1966 and also in 1968 Britten was involved with writing for children. The *Germini Variations,* op. 73 (1965), were not, strictly speaking, composed for amateurs but for two gifted Hungarian twin brothers, one a flautist, the other a violinist, both of whom were fine pianists as well. The variations, based on a theme by Kodály, were ingeniously conceived, enabling the two children to play on their respective main instruments as well as on the piano. *The Golden Vanity,* op. 78 (1966), is a vaudeville after an old English ballad especially requested by the Vienna Boys' Choir, who can hardly be referred to as amateurs either. *Children's Crusade,* op. 82 (1968), set to a text by Bertolt Brecht, was composed for Wandsworth School Boys' Choir and an instrumental ensemble involving pianos, organ, and several percussion instruments.

After completing his *Hölderlin Fragments* in 1958, Britten wrote no music for solo voice for some time, but he returned to the genre in 1965 with his composition of the *Songs and Proverbs of William Blake,* op. 74. The Blake poems are a song cycle setting for Dietrich Fischer-Dieskau whose unique interpretative style and color of voice was an inspiring challenge. So was the voice of Galina Vishnevskaya, wife of Rostropovich, for whom six poems of Pushkin, under the title *The Poet's Echo,* op. 76 (1965), were set to music.

In the writings of the Scottish poet, William Soutar, Britten found a like-minded soul, who shared his outrage over man's murderous inclinations and his concern for the fate of children who live in such a dangerous environment. Soutar's poems are short, covering the range from lyrical to nationalistic, including riddles and poems for children that he liked to refer to as "bairn-rhymes." Under the title *Who Are These Children?,* op. 84, Britten wrote a song cycle for tenor and piano on the lyrics, rhymes, and riddles of Soutar. It is one of his most concentrated and hauntng compositions in that style, near in stature to his settings of Donne's and Hardy's poems. Although Schubert is never far from Britten in his song cycles, on this occasion the stylized yet ghostly realism reminds one of some of Mussorgsky's song settings. *Who Are These*

Children? is no escapism into the world of innocent enchantment as in Ravel; beyond the nursery window the abyss is apparent.

The five *Canticles* for voices and piano (the third *Canticle* requires horn as well) all deal with religious subjects, but not in a liturgical context. They spread over a long creative period, as the first *Canticle,* op. 40 appeared in 1947, and the last in 1974. *Canticle IV, Journey of the Magi,* op. 86 (1971), and *Canticle V, The Death of St Narcissus,* op. 89 are settings of T.S. Eliot's poems, which Britten read with pleasure in the last years of his life. *Canticle IV* is set for three voices in order to illustrate the three Magi, and the whole work is made to sound strikingly Oriental. *Canticle V, The Death of St Narcissus,* which he dedicated to his friend and collaborator William Plomer, shows Britten's increasing preoccupation with death. So do his settings of medieval texts, *Sacred and Profane,* op. 91 (1974–75) for five voices.

In the last phase of his life Britten managed to create two more operatic works: *Owen Wingrave,* op. 85 (1971), in two acts on a libretto based on Henry James, and *Death in Venice,* op. 88 (1973), based on a short story of Thomas Mann, now made famous by the Visconti film. *Owen Wingrave* was originally commissioned for television by the BBC and was later arranged for stage performance. Consistently sticking to his pacifist creed, Britten once more took sides, albeit in an operatic form, in denouncing war and pleading for peace. Thus the opera can be seen as a parable against war. Yet there is a disturbing and unsatisfactory flaw in Own Wingrave's character since, in spite of his pacificism, when his bravery is challenged by the Ibsenesque heroine Kate, he falls into the trap of behaving heroically in the conventional sense, instead of defending his pacifism with a heroic gesture of cowardliness.

Britten's last opera, *Death in Venice,* op. 88, in two acts and seventeen scenes, follows Mann's story about a burned-out writer, Gustav von Aschenbach, who is on holiday in Venice. He becomes infatuated with an adolescent boy of great beauty and grace, Tadzio, who symbolises art, beauty, and love. By staying in cholera-infected Venice, he falls victim to the disease and dies in a state of acceptance and understanding. Mann's lifelong preoccupation with the nature of art and artists in the light of, and stimulated by, sexuality, disease and death, became in Britten's inspired music a profoundly felt last operatic testament.

In 1974 the ailing Britten composed his last orchestral work, *Suite on English Folk Tunes (A time there was . . .)*, op. 90, which he warmly dedicated to the memory of Percy Grainger, who died in 1961. Britten was not akin to the Vaughan Williams school, yet he had a profound understanding of and an individual affainity with folk music. It is of symbolic significance that one of his last works should be a creative vindication of the richness of English folk tunes. Moreover, the final movement, based on a tune collected by Grainger, has a swan song-like melancholy that seems to reflect not only Britten's earlier song cycle on Hardy's poems, *Winter Words*, but creates a foreboding atmosphere that was to be prophetic. Late in 1975, he completed his String Quartet No. 3, op. 94, in Venice. The last movement, *La Serenissima*, echoes the music of *Death in Venice*. His last finished work was for children, the *Welcome Ode*, op. 95 (1976), for young people's choir and orchestra. He died in December 1976 at his home in Aldeburgh.

His life was spent in total dedication to his art and the service of the community both at home and beyond. He was a conservative modern master who, like his friend Shostakovich, was a contemporary artist to the full, but without phoney avant-gardism. As a result he is among the few modern composers who offer a humanistic and immediate accessibility to the general public, but without compromise—the artistic integrity of Britten is never in question. During his life he received several honors, both at home and abroad, yet the one which, in a characteristic way, gave him the greatest pleasure was when he was made an Honourary Freeman of Aldeburgh in 1962. In his speech of thanks he said:

> I am proud, because this honour comes from people who know me. . . . As I understand it, this honour is not given because of a reputation; it is . . . dare I say it?—because you really do know me, and accept me as one of yourselves, as a useful part of the Borough . . . and this is, I think, the highest possible compliment for an artist. I believe . . . that an artist should be part of his community, should work for it, and be used by it.

The "outsider" wanted to be part of the Borough and became one through his labor.

7

In Search of New Sounds: The Continental Influence: Roberto Gerhard, Egon Wellesz, Mátyás Seiber, Elizabeth Lutyens, Humphrey Searle, Thea Musgrave

> With it [i.e. Serialism] music moved out of the world of Newton and
> into the world of Einstein. The tonal idea was based on a
> universe defined by gravity and attraction. The serial
> idea is based on a univese that finds itself in
> perpetual expansion.
> —Pierre Boulez

It is fair to say that several gifted composers did not find the directions taken by many of their fellow composers congenial. Postromanticism, nationalism, folk song revival and its influence, and neopast movements—such as Tudor revival and tonality-oriented conservative modernism—did not suit their temperaments and ways of thinking. They looked instead to the continental vanguard to find ideas and inspiration in modern compositional techniques that could enrich and liberate their musical thinking, as well as direct them towards new possibilities of musical expression. Some of these composers who emerged on the British musical scene started this process with an advantage, as they were foreigners who came to England as refugees from countries as far apart as Hungary and Spain. These composers brought with them, and carried on practising, those modernistic styles in which some of the native British composers were interested. As has already been seen in earlier chapters, most British composers followed the various continental artistic trends and movements with prudent interest and tried to introduce them, albeit often with a time lag of a decade or so. A possible reason for the delay was that experimentation in the arts and playfulness with ideas is largely a continental attribute, indeed tradition. The British, on the other hand, are by and large suspicious of matters intellectual and like to think "they know what they like," and what they like is, above all, the familiar—an attitude that is not conducive to experimentation.

The composers who have exercised the most notable influence on British composers in this century are Mahler, Sibelius, Debussy, Ravel, Stravinsky, and Berg. To this list the names of Schoenberg and Webern should be added, as their impact, both before and after the Second World War, was, to put it mildly, considerable. It was, of course, Schoenberg's dodecaphonic system or twelve-note technique that impressed even those composers who did not adhere to it, and Webern, who developed it further, opened it to new possibilities. This chapter is an introduction to those composers who chose to follow, even if in an eclectic, unorthodox manner, the revolutionary directions opened by Schoenberg.

Roberto Gerhard (1896–1970)

Gerhard was born in Taragona, Spain, of Swiss parentage. As was common with a young man of his period—and still not uncommon today—the family was very much against his becoming a musician. Indeed, they sent him to Switzerland in order to make him study for a business career. He eventually persuaded his family that music was his destiny. Returning to Barcelona in 1915, he became the pupil of two great Catalan musicians, Granados and Pedrell. His inquiring mind and determination to learn and widen his horizon beyond the Franco-Spanish cultural milieu, whose path usually led to Paris, made him seek to study elsewhere and to become a member of Schoenberg's class in Vienna and, later, Berlin. From 1923 to 1928, Gerhard studied under Schoenberg. As a result, during the 1920s, he witnessed and became part of one of the most exciting developments in the history of modern European music. Thus he absorbed, on the one hand, the Franco-Spanish musical heritage, including Spanish folk song, and, on the other hand, the Austro-German developments of the

time—above all expressionism as applied to music, leading to atonality and the serial technique.

After five years he left Schoenberg and returned to Barcelona
in 1929. His Quintet (1928–30) for wind instruments marked the
end of his official apprenticeship and was a parting bequest, a
proof of his craftsmanship in the old-fashioned meaning of the
word. A characteristically Gerhardian eclecticism was self-evident
in the Quintet: he did not follow Schoenberg's system in an orthodox manner, and he blended Spanish elements with the cosmopolitan avant-garde style.

In 1930 he married an Austrian, Leopoldina Feichtegger, and
in 1931 became Professor of Music at the Ecola Normal de la
Generalitat. This was followed by another appointment in 1932
as head of the music section in the Catalan Library. During the
Spanish Civil War, he was on the Central Music Council of the
Republic. The fall of Barcelona led to the exile of the Catalan
government to Paris, and the Gerhards decided to move to France
in the first instance. Meanwhile they contacted Edward Dent, a
loyal friend and president of the International Society for Contemporary Music. Through its activities they had first met well
back in 1932. It was with the help of Dent, who was Professor
of Music at Cambridge, that Gerhard was offered a "research
studentship" at King's College where he stayed to the end of his
life.

Gerhard's career as a composer falls into two convenient periods: works written before 1950, and the works of his maturity
from 1950 to his death. In the first period, the rich rhythm and
the Mediterranean color of Spanish music craftily mixed with
serial technique is heard—in many ways complementing the style
of Manuel de Falla. Falla's Spanishness, combined with an affinity
for Ravel, gained expression in the blending of the impressionistic
style with the neoclassical; Gerhard's Spanishness, on the other
hand, was a happy marriage of the fundamentally expressionistic
style of serialism. With both men, however, the emphasis was on
their Spanishness. Consequently, Gerhard's music did not get
stuck in the nightmarish groove of expressionistic mannerism as
was the case for so many of his contemporaries, including his
master, Schoenberg. Works such as the ballets *Ariel* (1936), *Soirées
de Barcelone* (1936–38), and *Don Quixote* (1940), the Violin Con-

certo (1942–43), and his only opera, *The Duenna* (1945–47), based on Sheridan's "Spanish" play, illustrate not only his inspired and masterly craftsmanship, but his Spanish panache.

The Violin Concerto, which is arguably the greatest accomplishment of his first period, is only partly serial. In the slow central movement, for example, Gerhard plays homage to Schoenberg by quoting the twelve-tone row of Schoenberg's String Quartet No. 4. The last movement, however, contains personal references in the form of quotations from the *Marseillaise* and a Catalan folk song.

The second period, from 1950 until Gerhard's death, opens with a set of further concertos: the Piano Concerto (1951), which received its premiere in Aldeburgh, and the Concerto for Harpsichord, Strings, and Percussion (1955–56). The 1950s also inaugurated his involvement with writing symphonies. His Symphony No. 1 was composed during 1952 and 1953. In this three movement symphony, the audience is confronted with a surprising procedure. The classical symphonic idea is based on the sonata principle, which relies on tonality and tonal conflict in combination with themes and which serves both the melodic and structural interests of the composition. Gerhard, following the theories of Hába, which he studied assiduously, introduced the idea of "athematicism" in his symphony—and he succeeded brilliantly. Instead of the customary use of keys and themes following the first subject-second subject exposition, development, and recapitulation pattern, he introduced extensive serially structured melodic units, which are in turn extended or contracted by rhythmic, tempi, and textual changes. The symphony therefore unfolds not via the manipulation and emphasising of primary and secondary materials, but by interrelated units of equal importance, such as color, rhythm, and tempo, which unfold in spatial time as one organic unity. Gerhard's desire for organic unity made him question the validity of the conventional partitioning of compositions into movements. After his Symphony No. 1, he progressed towards abandoning this tradition, and, in the last decade of his life, more or less all his compositions were conceived in one continuous movement, into which conventional movement structures were telescoped. This was a conclusion to, among others, a Lisztian preoccupation emulated and developed by Gerhard. In all he wrote four symphonies, of which the Symphony No. 3, "Collage" (1960), is a program symphony that introduces magnetic tape to enhance the evocation of images. Its setting takes place from dawn to night with tableaux of plant life, man, the unconscious and the conscious, and distant cities.

In 1964 Gerhard completed his arrangement of Camus's famous novel *The Plague* for speaker, chorus, and orchestra—a most successful composition. His Concerto for Orchestra of the following year shows the tremendous development Gerhard had made since his Symphony No. 1. The ideas germinating there have their apotheosis in this concerto and also in the Symphony No. 4, "New York" (1967).

Gerhard wrote many more compositions than those discussed here, but a surprisingly large number of them are not easily available, being neither published nor recorded. One is told that the Gerhards lived very happily, but one cannot help feeling that his creative genius may have been somewhat buried in Cambridge.

Egon Wellesz (1885–1974)

A Viennese by birth and education, Wellesz was fortunate enough to see and hear Mahler conducting and rehearsing; he inherited everything Austria could offer culturally. He was a pupil of Guido Adler, and, during the years 1904 to 1906, joined Berg and Webern in oder to study with Schoenberg. At the age of twenty-five, he met Bartók, who thought so highly of him that he took Wellesz's piano compositions to his own publisher. He met more or less everyone who mattered in intellectual circles in Vienna, including Bruno Walter.

In 1908 he was awarded a doctorate of philosophy for his thesis on a little-known Italian composer, Giuseppe Benno, who lived in Vienna during the eighteenth century. Having made up his mind to follow an academic career, which he hoped would give him time to carry on composing, Wellesz accepted his first academic post as lecturer in music at the University of Vienna, where he served until 1938.

His early compositions were written in the late romantic style and were mainly influenced by Mahler. To start with, his main interest lay in composing chamber music, but he soon developed into a formidably well-equipped dramatic composer who wrote ballets and operas, some of which were most successful. His musicological research in the field of early operas from Monteverdi to Gluck provided him with classical models. Several of his stage works are based on classical subjects, such as the ballet *Achilles on Skyros,* op. 33 (1921), and the opera *Alkestis,* op. 35 (1923), both to librettos by Hugo von Hofmannsthal. In his scholarly works Wellesz extended his research interest to the study of Byzantine music, about which he became a leading authority. He was the first to decipher the complex sign symbols of Byzantine notation. In 1935 he joined a distinguished group of scholars, headed by the Danish scholar Carsten Hoeg, in order to publish the *Monumenta Musicae Byzantinae.*

The annexation of Austria by Germany in 1938 suddenly ended Wellesz's continental career, and he sought refuge in England. Among others, it was Edward Dent who made the necessary arrangements for Wellesz to settle here, as he had for Gerhard. As a scholar of great repute, Wellesz was in an advantageous position, and soon a suitable academic position was found for him at Oxford. It was there that he completed, ten years later, his major work, *A History of Byzantine Music and Hymnography.*

As a composer, a period of silence followed his arrival in England, but, influenced by his own absorption with English poetry, he started composing again. The setting of words by Gerard Manley Hopkins entitled *The Leaden Echo and the Golden Echo,* op. 61 (1944), in the form of a solo cantata, illustrates the stimulating influence of the culture he discovered in his new country. More string quartets were also written during the 1940s. Some, like the Quartet No. 5, op. 60 (1943), based on serial style, display romantic nostalgia.

A striking and unexpected new development, however, was that the sixty-year-old Wellesz turned to the writing of symphonies. It was in the Lake District in 1945 that the idea of writing one came to him, theme and all. In a state of inspiration he completed the writing of his Symphony No. 1, op. 62, in three weeks. Between 1945 and 1971 he composed nine symphonies, following the great Austrian romantic tradition of Beethoven, Bruckner, and Mahler. Moreover, Wellesz had quite consciously set out to complement the Viennese triumvirate Schoenberg, Berg, and Webern, all of whom shied away from the writing of symphonies (Webern's Symphony, op. 21 [1928], can hardly be seen as a symphony in Wellesz's terms). Wellesz's musical thinking was not, however, modern in the sense of avant-garde experimentation. On the contrary, he showed more or less the same attitude to symphonic writing as he had to ballet and opera in his earlier days. In spite of his use of serialism, he never really abandoned tonality; indeed his vocabulary is largely based on Mahler and, to a certain extent, on Hindemith, whose music he ingeniously assimilated with Schoenberg's style.

Wellesz belonged firmly to the great Austrian cultural period which was destroyed by Hitler and his followers. His emotional and intellectual world was that of Stefan Zweig, Franz Werfel, Hugo von Hofmannsthal, Jacob Wassermann, Richard Strauss, Alexander Zemlinsky, and the Schoenberg circle. In Oxford, working as scholar, teacher, and composer, he relentlessly carried on dreaming and forging symphonies which echoed the European values that were so dear to him.

Mátyás Seiber (1905-60)

Seiber was born and educated in Hungary. At the Budapest Academy of Music, he studied composition with Zoltán Kodály, as well as continuing his playing of the cello, which was his main instrument. His ability was quickly recognised by both Kodály and Bartók—so much so, that when Seiber's wind sextet, the *Serenade* (1925), was not awarded the prize in a competition, Bartók resigned from the jury. His early works show the influence of folk music, as in *Three Hungarian Folk-Songs* (1922) for piano. Indeed, his catholic interest in folk music, which embraced Greece and France a well as India, stayed with him all through his life. His *Missa brevis* (1924) and the String Quartet No. 1 (1924) show the signs of Kodály's influence without being derivative.

His desire to gain experience and see the world took him to Frankfurt where he taught, played in orchestral performances, and was the cellist of the Leuzewski Quartet. For a year he even played in a ship's orchestra: this enabled him to visit North and

South America. A characteristically Seiberian feature became apparent, not only in his personality, but in his music: humor, or more precisely, wit and humor combined with serious craftsmanship in which no detail was left unscrutinised. It was this aspect, this sense of fun, that made him learn and study jazz. His expertise made him one of the first teachers of jazz at the Hoch Conservatory in Frankfurt in 1928. Works of the period running up to the early 1930s include two *Jazzolettes,* no. 1 (1929) and no. 2 (1933), *Three Nonsense Songs* (1927) for soprano and clarinet to a text by Christian Morgenstern, and the String Quartet No. 2 (1935). In 1935, like so many, he decided to leave the dangerous lunacy of the Third Reich and set off for England. For years he lived as a freelance musician, which meant doing everything he could in order to earn his living—from writing accordian tutors, to conducting (although conducting of a fairly unglamorous sort), to writing animated film music. During the war he was invited to teach at Morley College, where he worked for fifteen years. As an active member, he helped the cause of the Committee for the Promotion of New Music and, in 1945, he founded the Dorian Singers, through whom he promoted choral music of both the past and the present.

His reputation as a teacher attracted students from all over the world, and several of the then young English composers—Racine Fricker, Reginald Smith Bridle, Anthony Milner, and Hugh Wood, to mention only a few—were his pupils.

The String Quartet No. 2 showed Seiber's emancipation from Bartók and, above all, from Schoenberg whose dodecaphonic system he adapted freely. During the war he wrote the *Fantasia concertante* (1943–44) for violin and string orchestra. This was again based on a liberally interpreted twelve-note series. But the composition that is most likely to endure was written just after the end of the war. It is his setting of a passage from Joyce's *Ulysses* in which Bloom contemplates the starlit night, the universe and its vastness, as well as the infinite sweetness of things, coming to the conclusion that all is but an imagined utopia. Seiber worked on this cantata, *Ulysses* (1946–47), with total dedication; he felt an affinity with Joyce's work and found a sense of belonging. Setting one of the greatest modern masterpieces of the English language to music was an act of service to, and identification with, his adopted home and culture. The structure of the composition, which is largely serial—it even contains a quotation in its fourth section from Schoenberg's *Two Songs,* Op. 14—follows the five sections of Joyce's text.

His Quartet No. 3 (1948–51), which has the subtitle "Quartetto Lirico," invites the listener to think of Berg's *Lyric Suite* (1925–26). Whether this was accidental or a deliberate act of homage can only be guessed. Seiber also wrote numerous compositions for film and radio, of which probably the most famous is the music for the film version of George Orwell's *Animal Farm.*

His continuous preoccupation with the use of the serial technique, especially the permutational possibilities of the basic series, is reflected in the *Concert Piece* (1954) for violin and piano, which is constructed on the ingenious permutations of four-note units. In 1957, Seiber, an assiduous reader of Joyce's works, returned to him again by using parts of *A Portrait of the Artist as a Young Man* for his composition the *Three Fragments* for speaker, chorus, and instrumental chamber ensemble. Its three movements contain very atmospheric passages and a brilliant treatment of the words "He heard a confused music within him," which is given to the chorus, each voice singing in a different tempo with the instrumental ensemble adding to the general confusion. The permutatory technique was further polished in the *Permutazione a cinque* (1958) for wind quintet.

His virtuoso gift of being able to handle both so-called "light" and "serious" music, the two musical cultures as it were, is perhaps best represented in his joint effort with John Dankworth, *Improvisations* (1959) for jazz band and symphony orchestra. Frankly, however, it is one of his least successful compositions, as the blending is somewhat forced.

His last two works were his Violin Sonata (1960) and the ballet *The Invitation* (1960). In the same year he was killed in South Africa in a car accident.

Elizabeth Lutyens (1906–83)

One of the daughters of the architect, Sir Edwin Lutyens, Elizabeth Lutyens studied music both abroad, at the École Normale in

Paris, and at home, at the Royal College of Music, London. Possessing a private income, she was able to pursue her musical calling unperturbed by the often debilitating pressures of having to earn a living. She was very prolific and wrote—in addition to her main compositions discussed below—almost two hundred works for film and radio, as well as scores for plays.

A ballet, *The Birthday of the Infanta* (1932), based on Oscar Wilde's text and conducted by Constant Lambert, was her first significant public debut. The score was later withdrawn, along with a number of others, presumably because the composer felt that it did not fully represent her own exacting image of her progress.

Among several chamber music compositions her String Trio, op. 5, no. 6 (1939), stands out, with its striking blend of the styles of Bartók and of the Second Viennese School—Schoenberg, Berg, and Webern. This is a work that, together with the String Quartet No. 2, Op. 5 (1938), gained the approval of Elizabeth Lutyens herself, since she felt that it represented her early style and marked her development as a composer. The first of her five *Chamber Concertos* composed over a period of seventeen years (1940–57), shows her full commitment to the twelve-note compositional technique, a technique that she fully absorbed, making it her own vehicle of musical expression. In fact, Lutyens was one of the very first English composers who knew about serialism, and she practised it well before the public were even aware of the names of Schoenberg and Webern—a no mean display of dedication and artistic integrity. Similarly, the *Three Symphonic Preludes* (1942) and, above all, the cantata *O saisons, O châteaux!*, op. 13 (1946), set to the poem of Rimbaud, for soprano, guitar, harp, solo violin, and strings, illustrate not only her romantic expressionism, but also her sensitivity to poetry and her skill in writing for voices and chamber ensembles.

Even taking into account the String Quartet No. 6, op. 25 (1952), which was dedicated to Francis Bacon, the painter, and the *Music for Orchestra*, op. 31 (1955), her most striking composition in the 1950s was the motet in which she set statements made by the great linguistic philosopher Wittgenstein in his *Tractatus Logico-Philosophicus*. Elizabeth Lutyens, in her *Motet*, op. 27 (1952), succeeded in equating the revolutionary ideas of Schoenberg and

Webern with the equally revolutionary concepts of Wittgenstein. To quote the apt observation of Francis Routh in his book *Contemporary British Music* in connection with Lutyens's *Motet:*

> The musical characteristics of the resulting composition are precisely analogous to the linguistic characteristics inherent in Wittgenstein's text in the first place. It is one of the most apt pieces ever composed since the 12-note technique was linguistic in origin. Lutyens's motet is not a setting of words so much as a realisation of ideas.[1]

Even if the statement concerning the origin of the twelve-note system is taken with a pinch of salt, it illustrates most forcefully the intellectual brilliance of Elizabeth Lutyens's work.

Her marriage to Edward Clark was a bonus for her efforts at promoting contemporary music in this country, as he was a most far-sighted artistic administrator, who worked for the BBC. He had close links with several cultural institutions, including the Dartington Summer School, and was responsible for the promotion of many contemporary works.

During the 1960s, in the fullness of her hard-won compositional maturity, whereby, to paraphrase Luther's praise of Josquin des Pres's music, she was the master of the notes and not the notes of her, she wrote the Wind Quintet, op. 45 (1960), *Symphonies,* op. 46 (1962), for piano, wind, harps, and percussion ensemble, two more works in her *Music for Orchestra* series—no. 2, op. 48 (1962), and no. 3, op. 56 (1963)—*Music for Piano and Orchestra,* op. 59 (1964), and several exquisite vocal compositions that reveal her wide-ranging familiarity with poetry and literature. Her innate sensibility for words and lyrical vocal line served her in operatic writing as well. Her two early chambers opera *The Pit,* op. 14 (1947), and the tongue-in-cheek titled *Infidelio,* op. 29 (1954), were quasi-rehearsals for the three, more ambitious, stage works that followed. These were *The Numbered,* op. 63 (1965–67), based on the text of Elias Canetti's play *Die Befristelen,* in which, with Kafka-esque intensity, people know the exact time of their death and keep it secret; *Time Off?—Not a Ghost of a Chance,* op. 68 (1967–68), an intellectual tour de force, referred to as "a charade in 4 scenes and 3 interruptions"; and *Isis and Osiris,* op. 74 (1969–70), a ritualistic work about life and death. All her work, including *The Elegy of the Flowers,* op. 127 (1978), and the Cantata, op. 130, of the following year, are proof of her poetic vision, impeccable craftsmanship, and valiant fight for the cause of modern music in Britain. Her fascinating autobiography, *A Goldfish Bowl* (1972), while displaying an aggressive personality and justifiable anger, is evidence of her fight against hostile philistines. Her place in the history of dodecaphonic music written since the war is alongside that of Luigi Dallapiccola and Roberta Gerhard—that is, among the masters.

Humphrey Searle (1915–82)

Searle was born of mixed English-German parentage. He studied classic at Oxford while carrying on with his real interest, music. According to Searle's own recollection, it was hearing Berg's *Wozzeck* that made him interested in the nature of the music that had so overwhelmed him.

In spite of her parents' desire that he should take up a career in the civil service, he decided to continue studying, first at the Royal College of Music, where for a short time he was a pupil of John Ireland. In 1937, he departed to Vienna in order to study with Webern. After a year with Webern, during which he was engulfed in the musical life of Vienna, he returned to England and found employment in the BBC as Chorus Librarian.

At the outbreak of the war, the BBC's music department was moved to Bristol. There Searle had the good fortune to meet several outstanding personalities, such as Dylan Thomas, Lennox Berkeley, and the BBC Controller of Music-to-be, William Clock.

When he joined the army in 1940 and was sent to the Scottish Highlands, Searle found time for composing. Having discarded his earlier works as compositions of apprenticeship, he gave the opus 1 label to his composition of the Suite No. 1 (1942) for string orchestra. To quote the composer's own assessment of his style of composing:

> At this period I did not feel experienced enough to write strict twelve-note music, so I wrote in a kind of atonal style which was partly influenced by Bartók. Walter Goehr's concert began with Webern's orchestration of the Ricercare from Bach's Musical Offering, and my next work, *Night Music* [op. 2], took its orchestral style from Webern's ar-

rangements; I wrote it in honour of Webern's sixtieth birthday in December 1943.[2]

Evidently, the path opened up by Schoenberg and further developed by Webern was to be the musical direction taken by Searle. Together with Elizabeth Lutyens, he was the first British composer to implement, in a sustained and systematic way, the serial technique.

The tragic death of Webern in 1945—he was killed by a patrolling American soldier during curfew time—prompted his Nocturn No. 2, op. 7 (1945). On hearing this work, René Leibowitz, the leading exponent of serialism in France—as well as a theorist and the teacher of Boulez—commissioned Searle to write a composition for his chamber orchestra. The Intermezzo, op. 8 (1948), for eleven instruments, dedicated to the memory of Webern, was duly presented to Leibowitz, who gave its first performance in the following year. Searle was launched as a composer. His next important work was *Gold Coast Customs,* op. 15 (1947–49), a setting of Edith Sitwell's poem for speakers, men's choir, and an assorted ensemble of wind and percussion instruments including two pianos. This was followed by two more works of a similar kind: *The Riverrun,* op. 20 (1951), based on Joyce's *Finnegans Wake,* and *Shadow of Cain,* op. 22 (1951), which, like *Gold Coast Customs,* used the words of Edith Sitwell. The three compositions all form a trilogy of musical effects underlining texts that themselves possess musical qualities.

To this period also belongs the *Poem,* op. 18 (1950), for twenty-two strings, which was Searle's wedding present to his wife, and his delightful setting of Edward Lear's *The Owl and the Pussycat* (1951). This latter work illustrates the humor not only of Lear, but of Searle as well. The Sonata, op. 21 (1951), for piano, and the Piano Concerto No. 2, op. 27 (1955), like the chromatic Piano Concerto No. 1, op. 5 (1944), reveal Searle's lifelong preoccupation with the music of Liszt, of which he was foremost champion in Great Britain. His book *The Music of Liszt,* published in 1954, is a major contribution to Liszt scholarship. An interesting feature of Searle's musical thinking was his ability to blend Liszt's pianism and Bartók's percussive treatment of the piano with the twelve-note or just free atonal styles.

During the 1950s, Searle also completed his first two symphonic essays: Symphony No. 1, op. 23 (1953), and Symphony No. 2, op. 33 (1958). Both of these show his preoccupation and struggle with the problems of molding the traditional symphonic form with new compositional methods. In the same period, Hermann Scherchen, the great promoter of twentieth-century music and conductor of several of Searle's works, asked him to write a short opera. This request was fulfilled by the writing of a brilliant score, *The Diary of a Madman,* op. 35 (1958), on his own libretto and based on Gogol's famous story of the same name. Few texts could have suited the expressionist treatment better.

Most commentators seem to agree that one of Searle's finest symphonic works is his Symphony No. 5, op. 43 (1964). This is an unusual composition that has few parallels; it is a biographical programmatic symphony that sets out to depict, by purely musical means, highlights of Webern's life from his youth to his untimely death. *The Photo of the Colonel,* op. 41 (1964), his second opera, based on Eugene Ionesco's play *The Killer,* was commissioned by the BBC Third Programme and received its first performance there. His third opera (op. 48, 1965–68), his most ambitious but not necessarily his best, was inspired by Shakespeare's *Hamlet.* Searle based his whole opera on a tone-row setting of Hamlet's famous soliloquy "To be or not to be."

In the 1970s he created the orchestral piece *Labyrinth,* op. 56 (1971), the song cycle on Baudelaire's notorious poems *Les fleurs du mal* (op. 58, 1972) for tenor, horn, and piano, and several miscellaneous chamber and choral compositions, notably the Milton-inspired *Il penseroso e L'allegro,* op. 64 (1975), for cello and piano, and the fascinating choral and orchestral work to a libretto based on Thomas Mann's famous novel *Dr. Faustus.* In this latter work, through the fortunes of its protagonist Adrian Leverkühn, who is a composer, Mann created an allegory, not only of the artist and music, but also of our own times. In Searle's *Dr. Faustus,* op. 69 (1977), there is a conscientious cultural reaching out, as it were, to a distinguished line of predecessors both in literature and music: on the one hand, Marlowe, Goethe, and Thomas Mann, and, on the other hand, Berlioz and, above all, Liszt, whose *Faust Symphony* (1854–57) left a deep impression on many musicians before Searle, most notably on Gustav Mahler. It seems that the somewhat cosmopolitan nature of the Schoenberg system markedly encourages those who practise it to think in terms of wider humanistic issues, such as the condition and nature of art and the artist, cultural and European issues, and so on.

Searle's contribution to British musical life is considerable, not only as a composer, teacher, and writer on music, but also as a dedicated promoter of modern music; he was an active member of various societies and committees, such as the Soeity for the Promotion of New Music, the London Contemporary Music Centre, International Society for Contemporary Music, and the Liszt Society.

Thea Musgrave (b. 1928)

Thea Musgrave, a Scottish composer, born in Edinburgh, studied at the University of Edinburgh with Hans Gal, the distinguished Austrian composer, teacher, and writer, who, at the invitation of Sir Donald Francis Tovey, settled in Scotland in 1938. She also studied with the legendary Nadia Boulanger in Paris from 1950 until 1954. Thea Musgrave's musical provenance is thus impeccably founded on a sound traditional background. Her early compositions were tonal and largely influenced by Stravinsky, but without her adopting his neoclassical style. This tendency can be seen in her ballet *A Tale for Thieves* (1953).

It was through her association with the summer school at Dartington Hall in 1953 that she was first introduced to the music of the Second Viennese School. Her adoption of the "Sprechstimme" in her chamber opera *The Abbot of Drimock* (1955) shows the direct influence of Schoenberg in her music. This style was developed further in the *Divertimento for Strings* (1957) and in the orchestral variations *Obliques* (1958), in which the vogue for percussive instrumental effects is also markedly evident. Her chamber music is perhaps a more lyrical evolution from Schoenberg towards Webern's style, a style that dominated the young avant-garde composers of the post-war period. The free chromaticism of the String Quartet (1958) is left behind for the Webernian sound-world of her *Colloquy* (1960) for violin and piano and the Trio (1960) for flute, oboe, and piano.

Unexpectedly, in her *The Phoenix and the Turtle* (1962) for chorus and orchestra, she abandoned her Webern-oriented direction in favor of chromatic lyricism, nearer to her own temperament. Her next work in the same genre was *The Five Ages of Man* (1963). The oratoriolike setting of the text is based on Hesiod's *Works and Days*, a work in which, through the life of a farmer, the reader not only learns about farming but also about the inevitable decline of man. Thea Musgrave excels in providing the text, which depict's man's decline from better days to misery, with appropriate illustrative music.

Her second opera, *The Decision* (1964–65), concerning a miner trapped in a coalpit in Ayrshire, is less successful than her first; its episodic nature somewhat breaks up the continuity of the drama, and the suitability of the subject is perhaps questionable.

Under a spell of new creative inspiration, a whole series of various kinds of concertos emerged from her pen during the second half of the 1960s and early 1970s. The Chamber Concerto No. 2 (1696), while paying tribute to Schoenberg in its manner of scoring—it uses the same instrumental ensemble as his *Pierrot Lunaire*—is nevertheless under the spell of the American genius Charles Ives, whose music long fascinated Thea Musgrave. Among the many musical ingenuities characterizing Ives's musical thinking, his fascination with the superimposition and juxtaposition of diverse rhythmic and melodic elements was taken up by Musgrave. In her Chamber Concerto No. 2 (1966) is there not only the playing of "asynchronous music," but also, like Ives, several popular tunes, such as the hymn "All Things Bright and Beautiful."

The Chamber Concerto No. 3 (1967) follows similar lines to the second but in the third Thea Musgrave introduces a set of references to the names of several great composers via an ingenious fitting of relevant musical notes to the letters of the names of the composers. The sooner this hidden complication is forgotten, the more speedily the music can be enjoyed. Such devices are, on the whole, the private delight of the creator and as such they belong to the "mysteries of the workshop" and to the realm of the research student. In this concerto, however, a custom generally associated with jazz bands is introduced by Musgrave: each player is required to stand up when playing his cadenza. She applied this style of performance of her ensuing Concerto for Orchestra

(1967), the Clarinet Concerto (1967), and the Horn Concerto (1971).

The Scottish Theatre Ballet gave the first performance of her second ballet, *Beauty and the Beast* (1968–69). During the 1970s, two operatic works, *Mary, Queen of Scots* (1977) and *A Christmas Carol* (1978–79), demonstrated her wide-ranging and unfailing creative ability.

The largely folk song-oriented nationalistic school headed by Vaughan Williams's genius has exercised a noble and invigorating influence and has, without question, greatly enhanced the musical life of Great Britain. Nevertheless, it has an inherent danger of leading, especially in the hands of epigones, to an inward-looking, even parochial, manneristically pastoral and nostalgic style. Against this, an internationally oriented musical antidote in the form of the lingua franca of serialism was a welcome development. It is as a homage to those who have practiced serialism, often in the face of years of neglect and ridicule, that in its modest way this chapter is written.

8

A Child of Our Time:
Sir Michael Tippett

Chorus

Let us go down the hill with joy
To the bounteous life of this midsummer day.

All

All things fall and are built again
And those that build them again are gay.
　　　　—from Michael Tippett's opera *The Midsummer Marriage*

Sir Michael Tippett, although born in London in 1905, spent much of his childhood in the provinces and in grammar schools, while his parents mainly lived in France on the modest fortune made by his father in business. Music was appreciated by the family in the usual way, but the idea of their son wanting to become a musician was unexpected. The alarmed parents decided to turn to a professional musician for advice, and the dangerous task of crystal ball gazing fell upon poor Malcolm Sargent. His emphatic verdict was negative. According to the Italian philosopher and critic Benedetto Croce, one of the signs of genius is the ability to overcome difficulties. This Tippett has managed superbly.

Despite a relatively late start, he succeeded in 1923 in studying both composition and conducting at the Royal College of Music, but he was a slow developer and did not distinguish himself as a student for a long time. Nevertheless, he gained experience by engaging in practical music-making of all kinds. This gave him firsthand experience of the general repertoire, and he learned how and why the pieces he was rehearsing worked. To earn a living he became, for a short time, a school teacher of French—a language he had learned fluently during his many years of association with France. Although he had already completed his course at the Royal College of Music, he recognised his technical shortcomings, especially in contrapuntal writing, and decided to return to the College again in order to study there for another two years, from 1930 to 1932 under a much respected teacher and writer of text books, R. O. Morris.

It was during the early 1930s, when he was working in Yorkshire, that the miserable poverty-stricken conditions to which many people lived became apparent to him. He started to question the social values of his time and, like so many intellectuals of the 1930s who saw with alarm the rapid growth of the facist menace, turned to communism, believing that it was a way of bringing about a more just society. The failure of his attempts to convert his comrades of the British Communist party to the policies of Trotsky made him leave the party shortly afterwards in disappointment.

Works composed before this period have been discounted by Tippett as not being worthy of inclusion in his compositional output. The first compositions that have become part of his published works are, therefore, the String Quartet No. 1 (1934–35), which he revised in 1943, and the Piano Sonata No. 1 (1938), also revised later in 1942. These works already show the seeds of some of the now-characteristic features of Tippett's thinking: energetic vigour and an ability to write "fast" music, peroccupation, with complex rhythmic ideas, polyphonic texture, lyricism, and a tendency to incorporate the popular, that is, folk tunes and jazz in a highly sophisticated, modernistic idiom. The Piano Sonata No. 1 has a Bartók-like timbre to it—especially in the first movement; the second movement is based on a Scottish folk song, and generally the work contains aspects of Debussy and, to round off, Gershwin for good measure. Yet it is convincingly Tippett in style, and even today it still sounds fresh.

Tippett's first major composition for orchestra was the Concerto for Double String Orchestra (1938–39). Here his long studies of counterpoint and interest in Elizabethan music were brought to fruition. The work is, as the composer himself has described it, "a study in polyphony." The style and structure is a neoclassical revival of the concerto grosso style of the Baroque period: the three movement fast-slow-fast pattern favored by Vivaldi and Bach among others. The whole work gives an impression of inspired smoothness and natural flow. The slow movement introduces a lyrical tune that is partly folk/blues in character. Similarly, the last movement presents a folk tunelike theme that possesses a flow and an almost naive simplicity that gives the movement a sense of "naturalness." This naturalness is, of course, an inherent aspect of folk music, which Tippett had by that time assimilated both musically and ideologically. As for his popular-sounding tunes, whether composed by him or borrowed, they represent the democratic, humanistic factors via which he communicates with his listeners. In many ways Tippett is a "committed" artist in the best meaning of the word; indeed, he was one well before the expression became fashionable.

Tippett, who had already been associated with the musical activities of Morley College, London, was appointed to be its new director in 1940. He held this post until 1951, and during his time there enhanced the reputation of the College. In his first year at Morley College he created what is perhaps his most popular work after the Concerto for Double String Orchestra, his secular passion-oratorio, *A Child of Our Time* (1939–1941), for four soloists (soprano, alto, tenor, and bass), choir, and orchestra. He wrote his own libretto, which was inspired by an event in 1938 when a young Jew, avenging the suffering inflicted upon his mother by the Nazis, shot a German diplomat in Paris. The music itself belongs to the great English choral tradition. In contemporary terms, it stands in line with the works of Elgar, Holst, Vaughan Williams, and Walton, the latter's *Belshazzar's Feast* having a marked influence in several places. There is, however, a notable difference between Walton and Tippett, as Walton's great choral work is harsh and brassily pagan, while Tippett's oratorio has a lyrical and dignified mellowness. In the opening section, the chorus sings the words:

> The world turns on its dark side.
> It is winter.

At the end of the oratorio, after the alto solo, the chorus enters and repeats the soloist by finishing off with the words:

The moving waters renew the earth.
It is spring.

This leads to the singing of the last of the five negro spirituals, "Deep River." The spirituals are used in a similar manner to the chorales in Bach's oratorios, that is, they serve to exercise spiritual and emotional power by involving the congregation, in Tippett's case the audience, with familiar tunes. Of the work as a whole it must be remembered that in the early part of the war, many people thought that the Jews were exaggerating, in the same way as refugees from the Stalinist era were often thought to overstate their case. It is therefore to the moral credit, apart from the artistic merit, of Tippett that he was able to produce a moving testament of the human condition, so often characterized by some persecution or other, in which the Jew and all who are persecuted, including black people, are remembered. It was because of his deeply felt convictions that in 1940 Tippett joined the Peace Pledge Union, renounced war, and became an ardent pacifist and registered conscientious objector.

In 1942 he met Britten and Pears. It was for them that he composed the cantata for tenor and piano, *Boyhood's End* (1943), to a text by W. H. Auden.

Tippett's respect for Handel's music gained expression in his *Fantasia on a Theme of Handel* (1939–41), for piano and orchestra. Actually his work on *A Child of Our Time* and on the *Fantasia* overlapped. It is, therefore, not a mere coincidence that the structure of his oratorio deliberately followed the designs of both Handel and Bach. In 1942 he completed his String Quartet No. 2 (1941–42), in which he developed further ideas already apparent in his String Quartet No. 1, above all, the use of polyphony and complex rhythmic structuring characterized by a freedom that breaks the tyranny of bar lines. Of course, it was Beethoven's string quartets, above all those belonging to his "late period," that impressed Tippett and that he consciously used as models.

Nineteen forty-three was the year of his imprisonment for his "inflexible" pacifist convictions. He believed that it was with his art that he could and should serve his country, a notion that the great German composer Paul Hindemith had expressed earlier in the opera *Mathis der Maler* (1933–53). Once out of prison, he went back to Morley College in order to carry on with his work, which had been interrupted by the magistrate at Oxted. During his three month's imprisonment he had nurtured the idea of writing a symphony, and in 1944 and 1945 his Symphony No. 1 was written. It was performed for the first time in 1945 under the baton of Malcolm Sargent. In this, his first symphonic essay, Beethoven's dynamic symphonic vision clearly had an influence on Tippett's symphonic thinking, although aspects of Sibelius, Stravinsky, and, above all, Bruckner and Hindemith seem to have made a marked imprint as well. Many commentators have pointed to Tippett's interest in Beethoven's scherzo writing and its influence on him, but equally influential has been Bruckner's open-air scherzo style, as well as the neomedieval cadential points (apparently inspired by Perotin) much liked by Hindemith. The symphony has a relentless flow and rhythmic vitality; indeed, it is packed with ingenious contrapuntal ideas covering the range from sixteenth-century practice to the present, as can be heard in the first, second, and last movements. The composer's struggle for the musical *mot juste* and his process of molding of the material give a somewhat convoluted effect, so that the overall impression is busy. Indeed, there is too much; too many good things are going on. Already, in this Symphony No. 1, a characteristic profile emerges, which is both the strength and weakness of Tippett's musical personality—too much juxtapostion of ideas and trends drawn from all over—from the Middle Ages to the present. When the amalgamation of these diverse sources really works, as in the case of *A Child of Our Time,* wonderful things can and do happen, but, when on occasion there is no convincing integration, one is left with an emotional and intellectual Babel that is only redeemed by the sincerity of Tippett's humanistic conviction.

That Tippett decided to turn to opera after composing and writing the libretto for *A Child of Our Time* and after the completion of his dramatic Symphony No. 1 is not surprising; the great success of Britten's *Peter Grimes* in 1945 must have been challenging as well. Given his moral vision, it is not unexpected to find that Mozart's *Magic Flute* figures behind Tippett's first opera. Like Wagner before him, Tippett decided to write his own libetto, a task in which he had already succeeded in his *A Child of Our Time.* The theories of the famous Swiss psychiatrist and psychoanalyst Carl Gustav Jung concerning the archtypal images of the femi-

nine *(anima)* and the masculine *(animus),* the collective unconscious, the concepts of extroversion and introversion, and the
process of individualization in man's journey towards understanding and maturity found in Tippett a ready follower. *The Midsummer Marriage* (1946–52) is an operatic reflection on Jung's ideas,
which were increasingly preoccupying him. For those who might
want to approach this opera via a purely instrumental introduction, the *Ritual Dances from Midsummer Marriage* (1952–53) is rec-
ommended.

An incidental composition commissioned by the BBC during
the writing of his opera, the Suite in D, or as it is now known, the
Suite for the Birthday of Prince Charles (1948), is yet another example
of the way Tippett's mind works. The suite consists of five movements: the *Intrada* is a choral prelude for orchestra on the hymn
tune "Crimond," the *Berceuse* is based on a traditional French
melody, the Procession and Dance is a blending of the march
from act 1 of *The Midsummer Marriage* and an Irish jiglike version
of "All round my hat," the Carol is a medieval hymn "Angelus ad
Virginem," and the Finale incorporates material from Tippett's
Ballad Opera *Robin Hood* together with "Early One Morning,"
"Helston Furry Dance," and the composer's own folklike tune for
good measure. This strange cocktail of diverse elements, mixing
hymn tunes, folk tunes, and the medieval and traditional with the
contemporary, is a striking feature of Tippett's musical thinking
and philosophy. This philosophy is fundamentally humanistic and
all-embracing; cross-fertilization of ideas and events is prominent.
These ideas and events, however incongruous and unpredictable
they may seem at surface level, involving as they do the mixing of
blues and jazz with the work of Goethe, the Baroque, Jung, the
Nazi holocaust, Greek literature, and so on, find an aesthetic synthesis in Tippett's works in which a visionary quality of compas-
sionate belief in the dignity of man shines through. This
incidental, lesser work of Tippett is an illuminating example of
his style.

During the 1950s several more distinguished compositions
added to the steadily growing reputation of the composer. From
these, three works stand out. The *Fantasia Concertante on a Theme
of Corelli* (1953) for string orchestra was written for the Edinburgh
Festival during which the anniversary of Arcangelo Corelli's birth

was celebrated. It is a brilliant "neoclassical" work based on Corelli's own music, the Adagio in F minor. In the Piano Concerto (1953–55), Tippett decided to revive the lyrical element of piano concerto writing of the romantic period as exemplified by Beethoven and Brahms, but without the dramatic conflict principle of the nineteenth-century virtuoso concerto style. Instead, a dialogue between equals is created between the orchestra and the soloist. Harmonically, the work is based on the, by then, totally assimilated procedures learned from Hindemith and Bartók (that is, superimposition of fourths*). Some of Bartók's sound effects, as displayed in his *Music for Strings, Percussion, and Celesta* (1936), impressed Tippett sufficiently to make him use, in his ingenious way, similar effects in the Piano Concerto as well as in other of his compositions, notably *The Midsummer Marriage*. But the most outstanding composition of this period is his Symphony No. 2 (1956–57) nowadays referred to by some music students as the "ta-ta dum dum symphony" because of its percussive opening bars. It largely follows the neoclassical symphonic style of Stravinsky with which the Vivaldi/Bartók-inspired ostinato technique has been incorporated (see, for example, Bartók's Divertimento for Strings [1939]). Tippett's Symphony No. 2 follows the classical four movements scheme and is made all the more coherent by the bringing of the characteristic pulses from the opening of the first movement back in the Finale. It is perhaps a less adventurous, but a much more crisply concentrated, work than his first symphonic essay.

Tippett's second opera, *King Priam* (1958–61); like Britten's *War Requiem,* is historically linked to the 1962 Coventry Festival for which, with the generous help of the Koussevitsky Foundation, it was completed. To a certain extent his first opera, *The Midsummer Marriage,* is a modern relative of Mozart's *Magic Flute.* His second opera, *King Priam,* has among its influences that of Berlioz, whose own monumental opera *Les Troyens* (1859) inevitably comes to mind in the context of Tippett's work. Thus Tippett's two operas are in turn concerned with the archetypal subjects of love and war.

---

*Traditional harmony is based on the superimposition of thirds, for example: C-E-G, etc. Hindemith and Bartók introduced a new quality of sound by superimposing fourths instead: C-F-B, etc.

The famous legend of the Trojan War has two main interpreters: Homer, whose *Iliad* tells the story from the Greek point of view, and Virgil, who in his *Aeneid* tells us the story from the Trojans' viewpoint. Tippett based his own libretto on Virgil's story, in which the last of the Trojan kings, Priam, is eventually killed while the fallen Troy is in flames and at the mercy of the triumphant Greeks. Tippett employs a unifying "war motif" based on a combination of fourths (G-C-F$^\sharp$) that serves as a motto theme both melodically and harmonically. In order to symbolise and indeed create the tension associated with the violence of war, he used the augmented fourth (C-F$^\sharp$), which in the Middle Ages was called the *diabalus in musica* because of its unsettling and somewhat sinister sound. As the Symphony No. 2 is a clearer and better structured work then its predecessor, so *Kings Priam* is, in relation to *The Midsummer Marriage,* a better conceived and more concisely written operatic composition.

An offshoot of Tippett's preoccupation with the Trojan War is his *Songs for Achilles* (1961) for tenor and guitar, set to his own text. Such was his concentration on his opera that several other compositions written after the completion of *King Priam* bear its musical insignia: his Piano Sonata No. 2 (1962) and, above all, the Concerto for Orchestra (1962–63), which utilizes musical materials and sound effects found in *King Priam*. In more than one way the Concerto for Orchestra is a symphonic realization, a rich overflow of inspiration generated by his work on the opera. The overall structure follows the three movements fast-slow-fast scheme within which the instrumentalists are divided into small groups. These, of course, include the by then *de rigeur* combination of piano, harp, and xylophone, instruments for which he has a penchant. The two fast movements display an energy unusual even for Tippett. *King Priam* marks a happy period in Tippett's life, as he was temperamentally and intellectually on home ground, as it were, because of his long-standing interest in legends and myths, enhanced by his reading of Yeats, whose own involvement with myth fascinated him, and by Jung's theories founded on the recognigion of the importance and significance of myths. All these preoccupations helped to bring to fruition several compositions that reflect superbly Tippett's creative mind and visionary outlook.

It is the visionary outlook that gains full expression in his second oratorio, *The Vision of Saint Augustine* (1963–65). For its subject matter Tippett chose the *Confessions* of Saint Augustine, which he set for baritone solo, chorus, and orchestra. The whole work is an attempt to portray the ecstatic vision of Saint Augustine, a mystical vision of eternity that is shared by his beloved mother, Monica, and a seemingly next to impossible topic for musical expression. Yet Tippett succeeds in a remarkable manner in this work by relying on the very nature of music to represent eternity. Music works simultaneously at two levels as far as time is concerned—the mathematical and the psychological levels—and, at the psychological level, music can give the semblance of infinity. The abstract nature of music can, of course, be made more "comprehensible" by the use of words (this is shown, for example, in the humanistic gesture made by Beethoven in his Symphony No. 9), but in the case of Tippett's *The Vision of Saint Augustine,* the voices are abandoned in favor of the abstract nature of music, so that the composer is able to convey the complex mystical vision of the saint. The composer, who is well aware of this emotional and intellectual trademark, has declared:

> There has always been a visionary element in much of my music, which finds its first full flowering in *The Midsummer Marriage.* "Anything can happen" on that midsummer day—a day maybe that never appeared in the calendar.
> In *King Priam* too the hero comes to the "loop in time" and with eyes shut to the outside world, murmurs:
>
> > I see mirrors
> > Myriad upon myriad moving
> > The dark forms of creation.
>
> *The Vision of Saint Augustine* is a special case of the same expressive need.[1]

Tippett's third opera, *The Knot Garden* (1970), is again based on his own libretto. From the main subjects of love and war, which preoccupied him in his first two operas, he turned here to the subject of reconciliation. In the background of his first opera stands Mozart, in his second Homer and Virgil, and in his third it is Shakespeare who is the influencing force. The title page carries a quotation from *All's Well That Ends Well,* and in the last act—

there are three acts, act 1 "Confrontation," act 2 "Labyrinth," and act 3 "Charade"—there is a parody performance of *The Tempest* given by the characters, who include such figures as a freedom fighter, a black homosexual, and a psychoanalyst—Magnus-Prospero. The score contains the whole gamut of Tippettian musical expression, including his much-loved blues and a craftily conceived symbolic touch of bringing the hitherto discordant characters together by singing in harmony. He further indulged himself with his predilection for folk tunes, popular music, negro spirituals, and jazz by quoting not only from his own earlier music, but also from other composers. Again this major work resulted in a creative overflow in the form of the *Songs for Dov* (1969–70), in which a desire to round off both musical and poetic problems whose origins were in the opera finds expression. This song cycle for tenor and small orchestra could have been written by the young musician Dov in *The Knot Garden*, and a collage technique that includes Beethoven and boogie-woogie is employed.

For the Symphony No. 3 (1970–92), Tippett decided not to follow the firmly constructed path of his Symphony No. 2; he chose instead to surprise the listener with a work that in spite of its many fascinating ideas and fine orchestral writing, gives an impression of being labored and of being an altogether rather noisy and ideologically oriented piece of preaching. This is a weakness in him that, on occasion, such as in the second part of this symphony, can leave one ill at ease, in spite of his undoubtedly good intentions. The trouble with quotations (collagelike or otherwise) is that they can easily degenerate into over-indulgence. The second part of the Symphony No. 3 incorporates slow and fast blues with quotations from the Finale of Beethoven's Symphony No. 9, together with a Mahler-inspired solo soprano who sings a text written by the composer, which paraphrases Martin Luther King's immortal words "I have a dream." With that piling-up of emotive references, it is no surprise that for a while—like Herman Hesse, the German novelist—Tippett was made something of a campus cult figure with lapel badges and all. In contrast, Luciano Berio's *Sinfonia* (1968), which is a mine of musical, literary, and anthropological quotations, including an evocation of Martin Luther King, succeeded superbly where Tippett stumbled, because Berio avoided posing as a guru and thereby avoided the usually attendant schmaltz. Tippett's gurulike tendency is understandable and perhaps inevitable in a great artist and teacher who not only empathizes with the problems of the modern world, with the condition of man, and how it is reflected in the arts, but who also sees, as Britten did, that in spite of the stupendous achievements of British music during this century, the art form is still largely undervalued by those who should know better.

Tippett's fourth opera, *The Ice Break* (1973–76), follows the lives taken up in *The Knot Garden*. Again blues are utilized in a work that unfolds in an increasingly episodic manner. After the subjects of love, war, and reconciliation, which absorbed Tippett in his earlier operas, he turned here to the dual subjects of "stereotypes" and "individual rebirth." Into *The Ice Break* are telescoped not only several of Tippett's long-standing preoccupations and ideas about society and the condition of urban man, but also his experience of America, an encounter that has stimulated his imagination since his first journey there in 1965. The general impression of the opera is that it is a politically and sociologically oriented statement about our divided society in which human beings live a stereotyped existence that imprisons them and out of which a liberation is possible via the process of a Jung-inspired "individual rebirth."

This is a very concentrated and fast-moving opera, as the three acts unfold within the short time span of less than one-and-a-half hours. The staging and the episodic denouement, with its shifting and superimposed style of action, are more likely to be associated with film and television than with conventional opera. But then, Tippett is a breaker and rearranger of tradition.

The Symphony No. 4 (1976–77), commissioned by the Chicago Symphony Orchestra under Sir Georg Solti, is more of a symphonic poem following the Liszt-Strauss tradition, although Sibelius's Symphony No. 7 (1924), with its telescoping of the traditional form into one unbroken symphonic movement, must also have served Tippett as a model. It seems that in his later works, Tippett's ideas are scattered around in a nervously rhapsodic manner. His preoccupations with the dramatic continuity of "light" and "shadow," the Boulez-inspired "Arrest" and "Movement," the fast and slow blues, and so on, as manifested in his Symphony No. 3, have led him to create works that are fragmented and kaleidoscopic in effect and that do not always attain a coherent balance, but that nevertheless always suceed in enriching the listener with fascinating musical moments. The Triple Concerto (1979) for violin, viola, cello, and orchestra, for example, which was composed after the Symphony No. 4 and the String Quartet No. 4 (1977–79)—both of which represent a one movement cycle "from birth to death"—is a case in point. Its first two movements seem to be in search of an identity, but, from the third movement (which bears the indication "very slow; calmer still") onwards, the listener enters a world of exquisite sensibility and beauty. Here is one of the manifestations of Tippett's craftsmanship and the journey he has made from the traditional concept of thematic development to the technique of juxtaposition, which is one of the hallmarks of his musical thinking.

His thoughts in writing have been collected and published in three books: *Moving into Aquarius* (1958), *Music of the Angels* (1980), and *Song of Experience* (1991), which, like the librettos of his last two operas, convey noble and pertinent ideas covering a wide range of topics. At the same time, they confront the reader with convolution and woolliness.

The Mask of Time (1984) is a monumental choral work, a summation of more or less everything Tippett cares for, culminating in his strongly held hope that mankind has the power to overcome its own tendency towards self-destruction. Tippett as a musician of our time confronts his public with the age-old dichotomy of art, in which the aesthetic and the ethical gain expression. Finding the golden proportion between the two has always been one of the preoccupations of a great artist. The struggle is evidently there in Beethoven's music, a musician who has had the greatest impact on Tippett's thinking and whom, in many ways, he has tried to emulate. Like Beethoven, he too has recognized the spiritual value and real meaning of his art: that behind the entertainment lies a moral imperative. Or, as Simone Weil in *Gravity and Grace* puts it: "Beauty captivates the flesh in order to obtain permission to pass right to the soul."[2] Whenever Tippett's music strikes one as being temporarily unbalanced, it is always because his moral sense has taken the upper hand over the aesthetic. Through his art, one can contemplate his novel and visionary struggle, a struggle that is a testimony of our time.

9

The Younger Generation: Alexander Goehr, Harrison Birtwistle, Cornelius Cardew, Roger Smalley, John Taverner

> Good music isn't nearly as bad as it sounds.
> —Harry Zelzer

The members of the "Younger Generation" are, of course, not quite as young as they used to be. All those to be discussed in this chapter were born either in the 1930s or in the 1940s and therefore emerged into the British musical scene during the late 1950s and 1960s. One of them, Cornelius Cardew, died tragically in a road accident in 1981 at the age of forty-five. In contrast to such of their predecessors as Vaughan Williams, Holst, Walton, and Britten, they could count themselves as part of and the inheritors of a flourishing contemporary musical culture from both home and abroad.

They have had the advantage of being able to take for granted modern musical development, including those of the postwar period. Indeed, during the 1960s Great Britain and, above all, London, became one of the leading centers of music. The doors were opened, as it were, and the possibilities for experimentation seemed boundless. There was certainly no lack of encouragement, even if the public did feel bewildered at times at what they were hearing. A resurrected nineteenth-century German visitor could on no account have said during the 1960s and 1970s that Great Britain was "a land without music." On the contrary, music was flourishing in terms of concert promotions and in terms of the stimulating presence of the already established native and foreign masters, together with the up-and-coming new composers. It is worth recalling the fact that Pierre Boulez, one of the most influential French postwar avant-grade composers and conductors, chose to work in London, first as a guest conductor of the BBC Symphony Orchestra (1964) and later as their chief conductor (1971–75). His impact in promoting the cause of modern music through live performances, radio, and television can hardly be overestimated. Style trends such as *musique concrète*, electronic music, and above all, the dual, serial heritage of Schoenberg and Webern were, by now, taken for granted by the younger generation of musicians.

Alexander Goehr (b. 1932)

Alexander Goehr is the son of the eminent German conductor Walter Goehr who settled in England, as so many did in the 1930s, and worked for the BBC as well as at Morley College with Tippett, Seiber, and others. During his days in Berlin (1925–31), Walter Goehr studied under Schoenberg at the Prussian Academy of Arts. Thus the young Goehr inherited the legacy of Schoenberg's teaching and methods via his father. Schoenberg was in the family, so to speak, and as a result Goehr's compositional style maintains a Schoenbergian character.

As a student of composition at the Royal Manchester College, he became the founding member, with his fellow students Peter Maxwell Davies, Harrison Birtwistle, and John Ogdon, of the Manchester New Music Group, dedicated to the performance of modern music, especially the music of the Second Viennese School. Because of this, they are often referred to as "The Manchester School," in the same way, as say, the "Mighty Five" are in Russia. This is misleading because the Manchester New Music Group did not form a school in the sense of sharing the aesthetic ideology and sustained links that would warrant such a title.

Goehr went to Paris between 1955 and 1956 on a French scholarship; there he studied with Olivier Messiaen's master class at the Conservatoire. His return to London was followed by various activities, such as being a producer of music at the BBC, visiting Tokyo on a Churchill Scholarship, and being an assistant professor at Yale University, all leading up to a distinguished academic as well as a composing career, holding chairs at the universities of Leeds and Cambridge.

As a composer, Goehr's major influences, apart from Schoenberg, have been Webern and Boulez. Contrary to expectation, the influence of Messiaen is much less apparent. Goehr's Piano Sonata, op. 2 (1951–52), one of his earliest works, sounds like Schoenberg and shows how deeply he had assimilated the vocabulary of contemporary musical idiom. The *Fantasias*, op. 3 (1954) for clarinet and piano, on the other hand, is somewhat freer from Schoenberg's impact and also displays elements of the postwar avant-garde. This development in turning towards Webern and Boulez was made evident even more strongly in his *Capriccio*, op. 6 (1957) for piano. It is a study in post-Webernian style.

The work that made Goehr's name was a cantata, *The Deluge*, op. 7 (1957–58), inspired by Leonardo da Vinci. In the same period he also composed the piano *Capriccio* (1958), which he dedicated to Messiaen's wife, the eminent pianist and teacher Yvonne Loriod.

His second cantata, *Sutter's Gold*, op. 10 (1959–60), was commissioned by the Leeds Festival, but its atonal, violent expressionism dealing with the discovery of Californian gold did not capture the audience of the time. His Violin Concerto, op. 13 (1961–62), a more integrated and poetic work, is more accessible that *Sutter's Gold* for a first-time listener to Goehr's music. In the same year that he wrote the Violin Concerto, Goehr completed *A Little Cantata of Proverbs* (1962) for chorus and piano, based on William Blake's words, and the *Two Choruses*, op. 14 (1962), based on excerpts from Milton and Shakespeare. In these and in works following this period, Goehr's approach to serialism underwent a sophisticated change. He found the solution to integrating serialism with the techniques of earlier styles, for example, with the modality of the Renaissance, and he now used them confidently without sounding in any way imitative. Thus the not so little *Little Symphony*, op. 15 (1963), and the more ambitious and dramatic *Symphony in One Movement*, op. 29 (1969–70), are much more easily comprehensible than some of his earlier works—and comprehensibility, in purely musical terms, is among Goehr's most stressed desires.

His opera *Arden muss sterben*, op. 21 (Arden must die, 1967), was written in German and based on an English play of unknown authorship, *Arden of Feversham* (1592). It concerns the killing of a rich landowner by Mrs. Arden and her lover Mosby; this story was made somewhat Brechtian by Goehr's librettist, Erich Fried, and Goehr even succeeded in incorporating some humor, a rare thing in his chosen style. During the 1960s he also established and directed the Music Theatre Group. For them, he composed three short music theater works: *Naboth's Vineyard,* op. 25 (1968), which he took from the Old Testament and which he referred to as being a "dramatic madrigal" as it has an obviously Monteverdian affiliation; *Shadowplay*—2, op. 30 (1970), based on Plato's *Republic;* and *Sonata about Jerusalem,* op. 31 (1971), which concerns the false Messiah who deceived the Jews.

The principal idea of music theater is to offer short operatic works to both professionals and amateurs, preferably cheaply produced. Only a modest cast, therefore, and a small ensemble of instrumentalists is involved. There are also opportunities for singing, dancing, acting, miming, and technical (that is, lighting) effects, but in the case of Goehr, no electronic music, as he does not like it. There can be little doubt that his involvement with music theater stems partly from the influence of the ethos and music of Weimar Germany as exemplified by Brecht and Weill, and from American and continental developments of the 1950s and 1960s (such as the work of Walter Felsenstein). It also owes much to Britten's most successful *Church Parables,* written between 1964 and 1968, and therefore to a certain extent to Japanese theatre as well. This latter influence does indeed occur in the translation of the effect of Noh drama into his piano composition *Nonomiya,* op. 27 (1969), which, together with his earlier *Three Pieces,* op. 18 (1964), was written for John Ogdon, a fellow Mancunian.

Goehr's long-standing interest in Monteverdi's music was inherited from his father who was an ardent champion of Monteverdi's music, his father's edition of *L'Incoronanzione di Poppea* (The coronation of Poppea) and the Vespers of 1610 *(Vespro della Beata Vergine)* inspired Geohr to write a *Paraphrase on the Madrigal "Il combattimento di Tancredi e Clorinda,"* op. 28 (1968) for clarinet. The Prelude and Fuge, op. 39 (1978), for three clarinets not only illustrates his long-standing preoccupation with Baroque music in general and contrapuntal procedures, such as chaconne, fugue, inversion, and variation, in particular, but also his fascination with the color and versatility of the clarinet.

The earlier Piano Trio, op. 20 (1966), the String Quarter No. 2, op. 23 (1967), and String Quartet No. 3, op. 37 (1975–76), are Goehr's best and most mature chamber music compositions. The last two quartets, however, seem to be a return to the romantic serial style of the Schoenberg of the 1940s, combined with an academic composure. As one of the leading figures of those English composers who were influenced by the Second Viennese School, Goehr has turned out to be a much less radical composer that he seemed at the time of his cantata *The Deluge.*

Sir Harrison Birtwistle (b. 1934)

It was as a clarinet player that Birtwistle entered the Royal Manchester College of Music in 1952. Once there he decided to study composition with Richard Hall, who had been professor of composition there since 1938. The encounter with three other brilliant fellow students, Goehr, Maxwell Davies, and Ogdon, and their formation of the Manchester New Music Group, had a formative impact on Birtwistle. His interest in theatre and, more specifically, music theater and the dramatic relationship between music and words had its roots in that fruitful Manchester period. In 1960 he joined the Royal Academy of Music in order to study the clarinet further. After a series of miscellaneous activities, such as working as a professional clarinettist and as a teacher, he became the first musical director of the newly formed National Theatre in London in 1975.

One of the characteristic features of Birtwistle's output is his meticulous avoidance of conventional musical references. Not for him the symphony, concerto, quartet, sonata, or suite. Even his early wind quintet is called *Refrains and Choruses* (1957), the title underlining the fact that the musical utterances are influenced by and constructed on the models of dramatic and poetic texts. Accordingly, Birtwistle writes compositions, even those that are purely instrumental, with titles that have references to refrains, chorus, chorales, and verses and also with classical references such as Nouros, Tragoedia, Medusa, and the like. This reflects his involvement with Greek culture, which gains expression not only in choice of subject but also in his architectural interest in using balanced archlike patterns. His preoccupation with repetitive techniques and tone color is apparent in all his compositions. The technical sophistication at his disposal is, however, geared to the expression of violence and often quite off-putting brutality. On occasion he employs deliberate ugliness in order to confront the listener with dramatic ideas that are neoexpressionistic and deeply related to the theories and practices of Antonin Artaud's theater of cruelty, wherein the dramatist's aim is to cause painful disturbance in the viewer's soul, to make him see what he really is, or, for that matter, what society and beliefs really are. It is this principle that Birtwistle has, to a certain extent, adapted for his compositions.

One of the first and most illuminating essays in this genre is the orchestral *Tragoedia* (1965), an abstracted musical study of Greek tragedy, using extremely violent and aggressively vivid sonorieties. The *Tragoedia* was something of a purely musical dress rehearsal for his first opera, *Punch and Judy* (1966–67). This is a one-act opera to a libretto by Stephen Pruslin, who, apart from being a distinguished writer, is also an outstanding pianist specializing in performing modern music. Needless to say, this opera is not a Punch and Judy show for children, but is definitely a show for adults, presented in the form of a prologue, four melodramas, and an epilogue. In each of the melodramas, there is a murder, and four gallows stand ominously on the stage. At first hearing, the so-called "average listener" is likely to be put off by the violent intensity of it all, yet it pays to give the show another chance, as the music and the orchestral imagination displayed in it, as, for example, in the melodrama 2, are remarkable.

Commissioned for the 1969 Brighton Festival, *Down by the Greenwood Side* is a work for music theater, founded on the traditional British Mummers' Play or St. George Play, which in essence is a folk drama celebrating the death of the old year and the birth of the new year. Its English folktales and ballad-based subject concerning fertility and human life, including ceremonial killing, are carried out with menacing intensity and uncompromising individuality. His *Versus for Ensembles* (1969), one of his best instrumental dramas, using twelve players—nine wind instrumentalists and three percussionists—is equally violent in effect.

It was during this most fertile period that Birtwistle was also involved with the ensemble Pierrot Players, founded in 1967, and, when they were reorganized in 1970 under the new name of Fires of London, he joined a new group, Matrix. For both performing groups he has composed works like *Medusa* (1969), which requires electronic equipment. As opposed to Goehr, Birtwistle is fascinated by the sound possibilities offered by electronic music-making, as his *Chronometer* (1971) for an eight-track tape illustrates.

During the 1970s Birtwistle went through an Orpheic phase. Not only did he compose a chamber work for soprano solo and five players on that subject, *Nenia on the Death of Orpheus* (1970), but also an opera *Orpheus* (1974–77), which is something of a summation of his musical thinking to that date. Brilliant orchestral pieces were also created during this time: *An Imaginary Landscape* (1971), a discreet allusion to John Cage; *The Triumph of Time* (1972), an ideal subject for music and influenced by the painter Pieter Brueghel; and *Melancolia I* (1976) for clarinet, harp, and double string orchestra.

Birtwistle's music is highly individual and the most uncompromisingly avant-garde in Great Britain today. Influences, such as they are, come from Stravinsky, Varèse, and Messiaen, and from medieval music, above all Guillaume de Machaut and William Ockegham, but these influences do not overshadow his music and are not as readily apparent as they can be in so many of his contemporaries, who seem to walk in the steps of such figures as Stravinsky, Schoenberg, and Webern.

For years now Birtwistle has been outshone by the genius of Maxwel Davies who more or less dominates the scene with his dazzling creative personality. It is quite possible, however, that a better-balanced and more appreciative view of Birtwistle's achievement will emerge in the fullness of time.

Cornelius Cardew (1936–81)

Cardew started his musical career as a chorister at Canterbury Cathedral where he remained for seven years (1943–50). This was followed by studies at the Royal Academy of Music where he studied composition, cello, and piano (1953–57). A scholarship enabled him to go to Cologne, the mecca of avant-garde music at that time, in order to study electronic music (1957–58). There he met Karlheinz Stockhausen, the leader of the electronic avant-garde, and worked with him as his assistant. After his return to London in 1961, he studied graphic design, which he took up professionally. In 1964 he was awarded an Italian music scholarship for a year, which enabled him to study in Rome with Goffredo Petrassi. His early compositions, three pieces for trumpet and piano (1955), two string trios (1955–56), and three piano sonatas (1955–58), are indebted to Webern and to the post-Webern avant-garde composers Boulez and Stockhausen. But his encounter with John Cage, one of the leading American avant-garde composers, caught his imagination. Cage introduced Cardew to his ideas concerning such new compositional techniques as chance (often called aleatoric or indeterminate) music and the use of noises and silence. Equally stimulating was Cage's idea of making the performer part of the creation of a work by allowing him to choose or improvise possibilities as part of the rendering of a composition. Cardew's *Two Books of Study for Pianists* (1959) already show Cage's influence, as Cardew introduced new notations in order to indicate his musical intention, as well as giving complex instructions that stretch the performer's task of realization to the limit. With the *Autumn '60* (1960) for an orchestra of any combination of instruments and the *Octet '61* (1961), Cardew explored further this genre of compositional thinking, as, in each work, he presents the performers with musical materials which can be "composed" or "realized" by them in multiple ways. In the *Octet '61*, Cardew also uses "graphic notation," or "graphic score" a type of notation in which the composer introduces visual patterns in order to indicate aspects of musical events by way of analogy. These abstract patterns are visually amusing, in the same way as the French poet Guillaume Apollinaire's calligrams—his word-pictures—often are.

The ultimate step in indeterminacy taken by Cardew is his notoriously famous *Treatise* (1963–67), which consists of a graphic score of one hundred and ninety-three pages that gives no indication as to how it should be performed. Anything can be done, and anything may or may not happen—for example, it is possible to contemplate the score in silence, enjoying the patterns on each page. What Cardew is asking the performer to do is to "respond to the situation," and any response will do. As a zero response is also valid, the possibilities of musical and nonmusical responses are infinite. Through his involvement with the Association of Modern Musicians, Cardew gained even more experience in extemporised music-making, including electronic music of all kinds.

The setting of the first seven paragraphs of Confucius's *The Great Learning* (1968–70), based on Ezra Pound's translation, marks the beginning of a drastic change in Cardew's development. The work is intended for a large number of both professional and nonprofessional players and singers who are asked to respond to the various verbal and graphic indications more or less as they like. It was while rehearsing the work with students at Morley College that the idea of forming the Scratch Orchestra came about in 1969. The ideology behind the activities of the Scratch Orchestra was, to quote from Cardew's article in *The Musical Times* (1969), "A Scratch Orchestra: Draft Constitution," to eliminate "the barrier between private and group activity, between professional and amateurs." This theorizing quickly gave rise, in 1971, to the offshoot Scratch Orchestra Ideology Group, which professed admiration for Chairman Mao. The inevitable followed: Cardew started to write committed compositions in the spirit of the "Cultural Revolution" of China. A sample of the titles of his compositions will speak for itself: *The East is Red* (1972) for violin and piano, *Arrangements of Chinese Revolutionary Songs* (1972–73), *Bourgeois Songs* (1973) for unison choruses and piano, and so on. In the bourgeois security of a professorial post at the Royal Academy of Music, Cardew denounced indeterminacy and proceeded to make a critical attack on his onetime mentor Stockhausen in a book entitled *Stockhausen Serves Imperialism* (1974). Thus the carefree fun of decadent anarchy became superseded by the committed activities of oversimplified ideology. This was a great pity, as Cardew was a gifted musician.

Roger Smalley (b. 1943)

Roger Smalley's four years of study (1961–65) at the Royal College of Music were followed by further studies at Morley College with Alexander Goehr. Like Cardew, Smalley also embarked on a pilgrimage to Cologne where he studied with Stockhausen from 1965 until 1966. He became Stockhausen's ardent follower, putting his pianistic and general musical talent to the task of interpreting Stockhausen's piano as well as his electronic compositions. As a budding composer during the 1960s, he set to music a selection of poems, the musicality of which shows how refined his ear was in making choices of texts. These compositions include: *Septet* (1963) on poems by E. E. Cummings, *Three Poems* (1962–65) on texts by Hölderlin, *Elegies* (1965) based on works by Rilke, *The Crystal Cabinet* (1967) after Blake, and *The Song of the Highest Tower* (1968), based on works by two poets, Blake and Rimbaud.

During the 1960s he also developed an interest in the religious music of the Middles Ages and Renaissance. Inspired by the music found in a sixteenth-century anthology, the *Mulliner Book*—especially that of a minor English composer, William Blitheman, who was organist of Queen Elizabeth's Chapel Royal—Smalley composed a whole series of works in a style influenced by Stockhausen and Maxwell Davies, yet nonetheless individual. These remarkable reinterpretations of old sacred styles are fascinating examples of avant-garde religious concert music writing. *Gloria tibi Trinitas I* (1965) and *Gloria tibi Trinitas II* (1966), *Missa brevis* (1966–67), and the *Missa parodia I* and *Missa parodia II* (1967) confront the listener with an introverted intellectual integrity rooted in the past. This, however, is in complete contrast to the composer's own view; Smalley at that time arrogantly dismissed "traditional music"—that is, all who do not write contemporary music in the latest avant-garde style—entirely. One is reminded of the confident naivety of Tinctoris who in his famous treatise on counterpoint of 1477 dismissed everyone who was not born during his time—*Plus ça change, plus c'est la même chose*. Of course, these avant-garde sacred concert compositions do not present traditional types of settings, but rather a series of contemporary instrumental and vocal commentaries triggered off by Blitheman's themes. Accordingly, *Gloria tibi Trinitas I* is for orchestra, *Gloria tibi Trinitas II* for soloists, choir, and orchestra; the *Missa brevis* is a virtuoso *a cappella* composition with dramatic sound effects like whispering and shouting; *Missa parodia I* is scored for piano alone, and *Missa parodia II* for piano and an assortment of eight wind and string instruments.

. From the late 1960s and early 1970s onwards Smalley's compositional style and music-making became increasingly dominated by Stockhausen, so much so that his activities in Britain were to a certain extent an echo of what the master was doing on the

Continent. For example, the founding in 1970 of a four-man ensemble, called Intermodulation, with a fellow composer-in-residence at King's College, Cambridge, Tim Souster, is just one of the several acts of mimicry characterizing the period. One could justifiaby remark that the pre-Mao Cardew was something of a Cage, whereas Smalley is the Stockhausen of Great Britain. They are first-class epigones. The 1971 season of the Bournemouth concerts saw the first performance of a short-lived work, *Beat Music* (1971), in which the pop style is amalgamated with that of Stockhausen. It is as unconvincing as the Seiber-Dankworth earlier collabration involving jazz.

Monody (1971–72) for piano and ring modulator could have been written by Stockhausen. This is not a patronizing remark, but a reflection on the cosmopolitan, almost sterilized style of some of the compositions of the avant-garde that give an Esperanto-like internationality and interchangeability of expression. The *Zeitebenen* (1973) for four-track tape, was composed for West German Radio and first performed in Düsseldorf.

In 1976 Smalley received an appointment at the University of Western Australia in Perth. His compositional style, however, did not change, as his *Six Modular Pieces* (1976–77) for four flutes, the *Echo III* (1979) for trumpet and tape, and *Konzertstück* (1980) for violin and orchestra indicate. The influence of Australia is nevertheless reflected in his composing an avant-garde divertisement about the life of nineteenth-century Australian convicts—*William Derrincourt* (1977).

The possibilities that exist in creating and recreating sounds are just about infinite, and the search for the musical *mot juste* is the composer's craft and privilege, a privilege that Smalley takes seriously. The listener for his part should follow the advice of the American composer Roger Sessions, who wrote in his book *The Musical Experience*, "The key to the understanding of contemporary music lies in repeated hearing: one must hear it till it sounds familiar."[1]

John Tavener (b. 1944)

Tavener received his musical education at the Royal Academy of Music, where he studied composition and organ. Indeed, as a student he was already organist of St. John's church in Kensington, London. Soon after completing his studies he was appointed teacher of composition at Trinity College of Music in 1969.

Tavener differs markedly from the orthodox avant-garde in the dogmatic sense of the word. His music is not characterized by the inherent formalism of the followers of Schoenberg, Webern, Cage, or Stockhausen, but tends towards an expressiveness in which the often noisy sound effects do not echo a school of thought, but rather the desire to impress upon the listener deeply felt ideas and preoccupations, often in a rather simple manner. These ideas and preoccupations stem from his Catholicism (he has now become Russian Orthodox), with its inevitable mystical overtones, his preoccupation with death, and lastly his practical involvement with sacred music, which gives rise to sacred or near sacred compositions. Characteristically, it was dramatic cantatas that made his name in the mid-1960s; these were *Cain and Abel* (1965), based on the York Mystery Plays, for which he received the Prince Rainier of Monaco Prize, and *The Whale* (1965–66), which, apart from soloists, choir, and orchestra, also requires speaker, organ, and tape. These early works, influenced by the ritualistic and sacred works of Stravinsky, also owe something to Bach, as indeed do some of Tavener's later works, which more specifically reflect ideas from the B Minor Mass. A collagelike style characterizes Tavener's way of composing: he will represent a whole series of often vividly picturesque events. In *The Whale,* for example, Jonah's difficult exit from the whale is depicted, while at the beginning of this cantata there is the notorious scene in which an entry on whales is read to the audience from an encyclopedia. *The Birthday Bells* (1967) for solo piano was written for the celebration of Stravinsky's eighty-fifth birthday. It is a stylish homage paid by a young composer to one of the towering musical geniuses of this century. Stravinsky's death four years later prompted Tavener to write *In Memoriam Igor Stravinsky* for two alto flutes, organ, and bells.

Tavener's next important work was a response to a commission from the London Bach Society; the *Introit for the Feast of St. John Damascene* (1967–68), better known as *Introit for March 27th.* In the same year he also fulfilled a BBC commission with his *In alium* (1968).

The *Celtic Requiem* (1969) is hardly a requiem as it is largely a blending of such diverse elements as children's songs and games and the texts of Henry Vaughan and John Henry Newman (among others). There is also a contribution by popguns—a highly individual way of honoring death. The musical language is extremely simple. To quote the pertinent observation of Francis Routh, "It is, in this case, no longer a question of a composition consisting of the treatment and development of contrasting ideas of thematic materials; it is the varied treatment itself which is the composition".[2]

Several of Tavener's works show a predilection for Spanish subjects. Apart from anything else, this is because of his profoundly religious and mystical spirit, which finds affinities with Catholic Spain and above all with the writings of San Juan de la Cruz, the great sixteenth-century mystical poet and Carmelite reformer. *Coplas* (1970), *Nomine Jesu* (1970), *Canciones españolas* (1971), and the large-scale *Ultimos ritos* (1969–72), which takes for its starting point Bach's B Minor Mass, are examples of the fruitful encounter Tavener has had with Spanish culture.

Ma fin est mon commencement (1972) again reveals Tavener's theological preoccupation. In this work, like that of its great predecessor by Guillaume de Machaut, which served Tavener as a model, the principal religious idea that with one's death starts one's beginning gains a modern expression.

The frequent use of bells in his works in *In Memoriam Igor Stravinsky, Last Prayer, Lamentation and Exaltation* (1977), and *The Last Prayer of Mary Queen of Scots* (1977) underlines the religious atmosphere that Tavener sets out to evoke, although he sometimes achieves it in a rather trite way. All the above works demonstrate his interest in death—as do his *Little Requiem* (1972) and *Requiem for Father Malachy* (1973), as well as his *Akhmatova: Requiem* (1980).

His Opera *Thérèse* (1973–76) and the chamber opera *A Gentle Spirit* (1976) have not made the same impact as his perhaps still most immediately appealing work, *The Whale*. Like most English sacred music composers since the nineteenth century, Tavener can get schmaltzy, but his saving grace is his somewhat humorous bent, which comes as a welcome relief just in the nick of time.

10

The Conservative *enfant terrible:* Peter Maxwell Davies

But who shall know St Michael, who the serpent?
—From the opera *Taverner* by Peter Maxwell Davies

One of the most prolific and original composers who emerged during the 1960s was Maxwell Davies. His rise corresponded with the time when the influence of continental avant-garde (in particular, serialism) reached these shores in the 1950s and, having gained momentum here, arrived at its peak during the 1960s. In these circumstances, Davies became the unusually exuberant leading figure of the British avant-garde of his generation.

He was born in Manchester in 1934, and he studied both at the Royal Machester College of Music and at Manchester University during the period from 1952 to 1957. Davies was a contemporary and fellow music student of Birtwistle, Goehr, and Ogdon. The four of them set out to promote contemporary music and became generally known as the Manchester Group. As a student Davies was already primarily attracted to serialism, but it is noteworthy that his chosen subject for his degree thesis was Indian music.

His earliest approved composition, the Trumpet Sonata (1955), shows his involvement with rhythmic series, and the *Five Pieces* (1955–56) for piano also signal Davies's preoccupation with the fourteenth- and fifteenth-century styles of isorhythm. The medieval and early Renaissance influence is again apparent in his wind sextet, *Alma Redemptoris mater* (1957), which he based on a motet of Dunstable. This borrowing and modern paraphrasing technique soon became a characteristic feature of Davies's compositional style, which was taken up by several of his contemporaries.

116

One should not, however, think in terms of an evocation of the past in the style of, say, Vaughan Williams's *Fantasia on a Theme by Thomas Tallis,* but rather of a modern reinterpretation of old ideas and materials that are metamorphosed, often out of recognition, into a world of serialism and deliberate distortions leading to parody.

During the years 1957 and 1958 Maxwell Davies studied in Rome with Petrassi. It was during this period that he composed his *St. Michael Sonata* (1957) for seventeen wind instruments. In this piece, medieval and serial devices are combined with the antiphonal style of the Venetian renaissance. The effect is, however, of uncompromisingly harsh avant-garde sonorities. In the late 1950s the average conservative taste, as far as modern music was concerned, did not generally venture beyond the music of Vaughan Williams and Britten. It was a natural reaction that Davies and several of his young contemporaries wanted to go beyond what their predecessors had achieved and seek other solutions for their creative needs. These solutions were readily found abroad in the serial style of the Second Viennese School, as well as in the music of Messiaen and Boulez. Yet in spite of the deliberate reaction against conservative British attitudes, Davies nevertheless chose to rely heavily upon the medieval and Renaissance past, albeit in a highly original manner that still manages to *épater le bourgeois.* His iconoclastic avant-garde stance is deeply founded on conservative premises, and these help to make his music more accessible.

Prolation (1958) was Davies's first orchestral composition, and he was awarded the prestigious Olivetti Prize for it in 1959. The title is a technical term for the division of the medieval semibreve into either three units (major prolation) or two units (minor prolation). Thus *Prolation* is largely a work in which rhythm is explored together with note values and dynamics. As a result the music is more of a twenty-minute-long exploration of musical materials as such than a development of motifs and themes in the traditional sense.

Returning from Rome, Davies became music director at Cirencester Grammar School, a position he held until 1962. There he was fortunate in having a sympathetic headmaster who encouraged his work with children. The creative crowning of his singular

dedication to the cause of contemporary musical education, a
dedication that in simple terms can be described as Davies's ability
to involve children directly with real music, was his *O magnum
mysterium* (1960). It is based on four carols, of which the title
piece, "O great mystery," reappears three times. There are two
Webernesque instrumental sonatas incorporated as well into this
modal-serial melodic and harmonic mold, thus forming the following musical/architectural design:

Carol 1 Carol 2 Sonata 1 Carol 1 Carol 3 Sonata 2 Carol 4 Carol 1

The climax of this meditation in sound is the concluding organ
fantasia on *O magnum mysterium.* This concluding part is a strikingly original, modern organ piece. From the first part of this
composition, which is for children but does not compromise Davies' own style, one enters the adult world of the second part for
the organ solo. To quote the composer's own words, "Writing
music for young people presents certain problems—it must be
reasonably within their comprehension and technical ability, but
there can be no 'compromise' or 'writing down'—children would
soon see through such condescension."[1] It is a didactic masterpiece and one of Davies's most poetic compositions. It stands next
to Britten's *Young Person's Guide to the Orchestra* and Stockhausen's
Gesang der Jünglinge (Song of the young boys, 1956) in its originality.

During the early 1960s, while Davies was still teaching at Cirencester, the works of two composers seem to have engaged his attention: those of Monteverdi and the serial works of Stravinsky's late
period. It was above all Monteverdi's Vespers of 1610 *(Vespro della
Beata Vergine)* that inspired three compositions: the String Quartet (1961), *Leopardi Fragments* (1961) for soprano, contralto and
chamber ensemble, and *Sinfonia* (1962). All three works are characterized by the mellowing presence of thirds and sixths, which
enables Davies to bring to the fore his lyricism and sensuous
warmth that lurk behind even his most daring compositions. In
his individual way Davies is a romantic at heart, and although he
lives in a different emotional and intellectual world from Berg,
he nevertheless shares Berg's lyrical romantic expressionism,
which he enriches further with carefully cultivated mysticism. Of

these three works, the *Sinfonia,* consisting of four movements, is perhaps the most deeply related to Monteverdi's Vespers of 1610, and, of their relationship to Monteverdi, Davies wrote that they "are variations on the Monteverdi original in the sense of Picasso's pictures based on a Goya original."[2]

In 1962 Davies went to Princeton on a Fellowship, staying there until 1964. During this time he completed or developed further a remarkable set of compositions, all of which were largely inspired by the great sixteenth-century English master John Taverner. Taverner was a significant composer and organist of his time, but is best remembered for three things: his Mass based on a secular song *The Western Wynde,* for his instrumental transcription of the *In Nomine* from another of his eight masses *(Gloria tibi Trinitas),* and, finally, because he was jailed for heresy in 1528 and apparently abandoned music after his release. Davies's germinating idea was to write an opera on Taverner's life. This was already in Davies's workshop in 1957, as it were, but it took several compositions and many years to reach the final goal. Meanwhile, in the year of his departure for America, the *First Fantasia on an In Nominee of John Taverner* was completed and given its first performance at the 1962 Promenade Concerts. In it, Davies revived the English *In nomine* tradition of transcribing these themes for instruments—the tradition probably started by Taverner and abandoned by Purcell's time. This work was followed by a short suite, *Seven In Nomines* (1963–65), for chamber ensemble, which the composer regarded: "as studies for a large orchestral work commissioned by the London Philharmonic Orchestra, which I had decided to base on John Taverner's *In Nomine.* In this way I could prepare an experiment with the basic material of the orchestral piece."[3] The large orchestral work referred to was his *Second Fantasia on John Taverner's In Nomine,* which was completed in 1964 and first performed at the Royal Festival Hall in the following year. Based on Davies's then incomplete opera *Taverner,* it takes the music from the completed first act. It consists of thirteen sections that are played without pause and lasts forty minutes. This was his most ambitious orchestral work since *Prolation* and shows a complete fusion of the modern with medieval and Renaissance technical procedures and styles. Indeed, it could be argued that, in Davies's music, one is confronted with a contemporary

stylistic development as important as neoclassicism. Davies's inno-
vation is a neomedieval/Renaissance style that seems to go perhaps
even deeper in amalgamating the two styles of past and present.
The interaction of the post-Webern and postmodernist approach
with the medieval/Renaissance element in his works gains a cohesion that, on occasion, seems more convincing than the often superficial tendencies of the neoclassicists, in whose works the *"jeux"*
elements often had the upper hand. Although Davies has hardly
anything to do with Bartók, nevertheless in his concentrated intensity of blending the past with the present, he shows a not dissimilar singlemindedness. He has explained his compositional
intention in the large-scale symphonic work, the *Second Fantasia,*
as follows:

> The musical processes involved are perhaps somewhat analogous to
> the literary techniques employed by Hoffman in, say, *Meister Floh,*
> where certain people, spirits and plants are shown to be, within the
> context of an elaborate "plot," manifestations of the same character-
> principle—as is made clear by a line of connection (not a process of
> development!) that is sometimes semantic.[4]

In addition to the influence of the distant past and avant-garde
present, it is possible to detect the influence of Mahler's symphonies in the *Second Fantasia,* as commentators such as Pruslin, Arnold, and Griffiths have remarked, although this influence is
almost purely structural. Davies was moving in directions where
Britten before him had made at least fleeting visits; they have a
greater affinity than superficially meets the ear. Davies's *Second
Fantasia* is a fine accomplishment, and it gave a clear indication
of the emergence of a modern symphonist on the British musical scene.

The American period also includes, among other works, the
Veni Sancte Spiritus (1963) for three-part choir (soprano, alto, and
bass) and chamber orchestra, in which sophisticated contrapuntal
devices, such as canon, diminution, inversion, and the medieval
hocket style favoured by Machaut, are ingeniously incorporated
to brilliant effect. The stay in America was followed by more travel
as a lecturer in music and musical education and as a composer
both in Europe and the Commonwealth: Canada, Australia, and
New Zealand.

Davies's return to Britain was marked by the formation of a

chamber emsemble, the Pierrot Players, that he and Birtwistle together directed until they split up in 1970. Davies then formed his own group, the Fires of London. Since its formation this ensemble has become a vehicle for performing many and, from 1970, most of Davies's compositions. Several of these are works for the music theater genre with which both Davies and Birtwistle became involved. It is difficult to define the nature of music theater because of its flexible nature. In essence it involves a type of composition that can be operatic, but that is more often than not a concert piece with part staging, acting, and singing. One of its characteristic features, apart from cruelty (which has already been touched upon in chapter 9), is the emphatic practice of parody. To this genre of composition belong several works of Davies. In *Revelation and Fall* (1965–66) he frighteningly evokes the quasi-surrealist and early expressionist, menancing world of the Austrian poet George Trakle, who ended his life insane and committed suicide after his experiences in the First World War. Davies uses grotesque parody of dance music when dealing with Trakle's theme of death and backs it with strong visual effects and screams. With the *Missa Super L'homme armé* (1968), based on a fifteenth-century anonymous mass setting of the famous secular French song *The Armed Man,** Davies introduces the concept of musical blasphemy. In his own explanatory note, the composer draws an analogy between Joyce's techniques in *Ulysses* and his own in an illuminating way:

> The eventual treatment stems from the chapter in the *Ulysses* of Joyce corresponding to the Cyclops chapter in *Homer.* In the Joyce, a conversation in a tavern is interrupted by insertions which seize upon a small, passing idea in the main narrative and amplify this, often out of all proportion, in a style which bears no relationship to the style of the germinal idea which sparked off the insertion. The insertion is often itself a parody—of a newspaper account of a fashionable wedding, or of the Anglican Creed, for instance.[5]

Thus the incomplete fifteenth-century *Agnus Dei* is strikingly

---

*L'homme armé: the original text reads: "One must be on guard against the soldier. Everywhere it has been announced that everybody should arm himself with an iron hauberk" (A. T. Davidson and W. Apel, *Historical Anthology of Music* [Cambridge: Harvard University Press, 1978], 7:248).

modified by the introduction of new, alien materials that create distortion and stylistic juxtapositions and confrontations. Herein lies the musical blasphemy as such, as the sacred object is parodied, if not raped, by the insertions of incongruous musical materials that, on occasions, make a mockery of the original *Agnus Dei*, and by confrontations such as, for example, a pseudo-Victorian hymn, prerecorded music on a 78 r.p.m. disc with a sticking needle, and the incorporation of an automatic piano. The result is a work that is immensely serious and at the same time wickedly hilarious. The danger of reducing the music to the style of a Ken Russell entertainment is just about tastefully avoided. The danger, however, is there all the same.

The work that is perhaps best conceived for the purpose of music theater is *Eight Songs for a Mad King* (1969). It is, of course, linked closely with Schoenberg's melodrama *Pierrot Lunaire* (1912) in its instrumentation and expressionistic style, as well as in certain similarities with the alienated protagonist, the Mad King. But whereas, with *Pierrot,* one is allowed to know that Pierrot is Pierrot, regardless of whether he is interpreted in the first or third persons, with Davies's work, the listener is left in suspense, because one does not know whether the Mad King (George III) really is the king or merely somebody who imagines himself to be the king. Davies's idea that the Mad King should try to make the mechanical birds sing the music that he hears in his head challenged him to use both instrumental and vocal effects that are startling. In order to understand the composer's complex thinking and intentions it is well worth considering his own comments for the *Eight Songs for a Mad King:*

> The climax of the work is the end of No. 7, where the King snatches the violin through the bars of the player's cage and breaks it. This is not just the killing of a bullfinch—it is a giving-in to insanity, and a ritual murder by the King of a part of himself, after which, at the beginning of No. 8, he can announce his own death.[6]

Several more works were subsequently written by Davies for music theatre, of which the poetic *Le jongleur de Notre Dame* (1978) and *Cinderella* (1980), both written for children, stand out. The genre has singularly suited his temperament and way of writing dramatic chamber works. In these works he is able to exercise his inclination for borrowing, parody, satire, distortion, and musical blasphemy. Directed by his unfailing instinct for the musico-dramatic, he has brought forth the musical equivalent of the theater of the absurd. It has given him a free hand to experiment with unexpected sound combinations that are often achieved by introducing a medley of instruments and equipment used as instruments, from honky-tonk piano, bells, and old gramophone records, to the didgeridoo (an instrument used by the Australian aborigines).

Nineteen sixty-nine was a particularly fruitful year for the composer; over and above the stupendous *Eight songs for a Mad King,* he also completed some small compositions and two large-scale orchestral works: *Worldes Blis* (1966–69) and *St. Thomas Wake— Foxtrot for Orchestra.*

The *Worldes Blis* is a motet for orchestra that moves in a slow pace for a time span of some forty minutes. In it the composer maps out in purely musical terms his impression of the Orkney Islands' landscape. In the early 1970s he made his sanctuary on Hoy, one of these far northern Scottish islands. The composer's own notes reveal the close personal relationship between his life and music:

> bearing in mind that ultimately one's music and one's life are insepa-rably interrelated, I had in its form defined, in a way which made immediate and instinctive sense, the future environment in which I was to compose, when the music, as it were, materialised into a physical landscape. It could well help the listener unfamiliar with its style to relate its architecture to the slowing rolling treeless landscape. . . . Or-kney's wildest island seems to be a natural extension and a living-out of the territory explored and cartographed in *Worldes Blis.*[7]

In *St. Thomas Wake—Foxtrot for Orchestra* (1969), an original pavan (a popular dance form of the sixteenth and seventeenth centuries) of the great English keyboard composer John Bull is not so much parodied, as equated with an equally popular dance form of the current century, the foxtrot. Thus the old-time popular and the modern popular reinforce each other in a perpetual dance of past and present.

Vesalii icones (1969) is a work that, although written for music theater, might well be considered separately because of also being a strange combination of dance, solo concerto, and suitelike genres for cello and small instrumental ensemble. The inspiration behind this medley that has, nevertheless, been molded into an organic whole, was *De Humani Corporis Fabrica* by the Flemish anatomist Andreas Vesalius. His work, the *Structure of the Human Body* (in seven books), published in 1543, contains accurate descriptions of the human anatomy and was bought in a facsimile edition by Davies. Inspired by the illustrations in the book, he decided to write a series of dances depicting the anatomical illustrations. Then he thought of superimposing religious ideas—the Stations of the Cross and the Resurrection—leading back to the dancer's exploration of his own body in terms of Vesalius's illustrations. Thus the dancer's dance becomes a reenactment of Calvary both in personal and symbolic terms; the Vesalius illustrations serve as a series of emblemlike illustrations of *Ecce homo*. Accordingly, the music also operates at three levels: plainsong, "popular" music, and Davies's own contemporary style. In the closing section there is, however, an unexpected twist, but with a moral. To quote the composer again:

> In the last dance, "The Resurrection," the Christ story is modified. It is the Antichrist—the dark "double" of Christ of medieval legend, indistinguishable from the "real" Christ—who emerges from the tomb and puts his curse on Christendom to all eternity. Some may consider such an interpretation sacrilegious—but the point I am trying to make is a moral one—it is a matter of distinguishing the false from the real—that one should not be taken in by appearances.[8]

The instrumental ensemble, together with the solo cello part, gives the abstracted commentaries; indeed the cello can be seen as the spiritual partner of the dancer in a sense of a physical and spiritual *pas de deux*.

Since 1970 Davies has lived on-and-off in Scotland on his much-loved island of Hoy in the Orkneys. It is there that he ventured to write music for the films of the notorious *enfant terrible* of the film industry, Ken Russell. He wrote music for the films *The Devils* (1970) and *The Boy Friend* (1971); both scores reflect the preoccupations of his other works. Pastiche, parody, satire, and expressionist sexuality all blend in well with Russell's own artistic vision.

It was in 1972 that Covent Garden put on Davie's long-awaited opera *Taverner* (1972). It was well over a decade since he had first thought of writing an opera on Taverner, during which time he had composed several compositions related to it. As has already been seen, these were created as studies or forerunners to the opera. It is therefore something of a culmination of Davies's dramatic writings in which he unfolds, in two acts (eight scenes in all), the life as well as the intellectual and moral dilemma of the protagonist, John Taverner. This is a singularly dark and forceful work. Perhaps the nearest contemporary precedent is Hindemith's *Mathis der Maler* (1934), in which the artist is also confronted with the dilemma of loyalty to his art versus his religious and social commitment. Here the similarities more or less end, however, as the two composers' musical styles are miles apart. Davies's nightmarish parodies and his introduction of a jester who turns out to be death himself give the drama greater excitement; in Davies's *Taverner* the actions move with a relentless élan. Hindemith, on the other hand, is heavy-going, as he preaches a little too much.

Davies's affinity with the Orkneys, not unlike Bax's relationship with Ireland, is not just based on the romantic notion of wanting to be away from it all in peace and solitude. His escape to Scotland has proved to be an encounter with values, Scottish cultural values, which have stimulated his creative imagination and which have led him to find his own "Borough," in the same way Britten did earlier in Aldeburgh. It is telling that he has set up the St. Magnus Festival in Kirkwall and Stromness, making it a counterpart to the annual festival at Aldeburgh. Over and above the landscape, the sea, and the solitude and the finding of a "Borough" and Scottish music, it has been Davies's encounter there with Scottish literature and, above all, with the writings of the distinguished poet, playwright, novelist, and short story writer George Mackay Brown that have influenced him. Brown was born and brought up in Orkney, and most of his writings are deeply rooted in Orcadian folklore and rural life. Davies has set several of his works to music, among them: *From Stone to Thorn* (1971) for mezzo-soprano, basset clarinet, guitar, harpsichord, and percussion; *Dark Angels* (1974) for guitar and soprano; *The Blind Fiddler* (1975) for soprano, flute, clarinet, keyboard, guitar, percussion, violin, and cello; *The Martyrdom of St. Magnus* (1976), a chamber opera for five singers and ten players; and the splendid cantata *Into the Labyrinth* (1983). These are sufficient to demonstrate the impact of Brown's writings. Moreover, Scottish musical culture of the past is also drawn upon in his stylish setting of *Renaissance Scottish Dances* (1973), taken from the volume of *Early Scottish Music* in the *Musica Brittanica*, as well as from *Scottish Keyboard Music*, both compiled and edited by the Scottish scholar Kenneth Elliott. The setting of Psalm 124 (1974), with its harmonium imitation and guitar recitative, is similarly based on music taken from the *Early Scottish Music*.

Living on Hoy has put Davies in close proximity with nature and with the sea. This has had a generally expansive influence on his music; he has increasingly turned to larger-scale compositions, such as the symphony, in which, according to some commentators and the composer's own statements, the vastness of the sea, the long horizons, and the bleak landscape seem to have affected his orchestra and even solo instrumental writings. The three symphonies and the Piano Sonata would seem to bear out this interpretation.

Inspiration drawn from one of Brown's poems about a deserted Orkney valley grew into the Symphony No. 1 (1975–76). The other acknowledged influences were Sibelius's Symphony No. 5, as well as Schumann's Symphony No. 2. and Boulez's *Pli selon pli.* The composer has gone out of his way (as in all his notes) to guide the listener in the right direction.

> Perhaps it would help to put listeners in a frame of mind sympathetic to at least the intention, if not the result of this work, to know that possibly the creative artists I admire most are two medieval writers, whose language to my mind, builds the only sound structures parallel to the statement made by the medieval cathedrals—Dante and St Thomas Aquinas.[9]

If the germinating idea of the Symphony No. 1 was ". . . the ruined and deserted crofts in an Orkney valley," via Brown's poem, the Symphony No. 2 (1980) was born out of observing the sea. Again we can turn to the graphic description of the composer:

> At the foot of the cliff below my window the Atlantic and the North Sea meet, with all the complex interweaving of currents and wave shapes, and the conflicts of weather that such an encounter implies. . . .
> I had observed two basic wave-types of potential interest—that

where the wave-shape moves through the sea while the water remains
(basically) static—as when breakers roll in towards a shoreline (moving
form, static content of wave)—and that where the wave-shape is static
and constant, while the water moves through it—as when an obstacle,
a sea-wreck, for example, protrudes through the surface of a tide race,
making a placid wave-shape behind it (static form, moving content).

While I was first working on the musical possibilities in these two
extremely different yet related wave-patterns and various interactions
between them, I came upon André Gide's exact observation of the
same phenomenon, noted in an early diary, while on holiday on
France's north coast, and also upon Leonardo da Vinci's precise
sketches of both wave types.

These two formulations governed the composition of the new symphony, in small architectural detail and also in long time spans over
whole movements, and more.[10]

Although it is not immediately apparent, the Symphony No. 2 is
tonal. It is in B minor, and the E sharp used in it functions as an
alternative dominant instead of the traditionally expected F sharp.
This guarantees tension as it is a tritone (augmented fourth or
diminished fifth), which was referred to as the "devil in music"
during the Middle Ages on account of its sinister sound. The
composer has, however, been quick to explain that "there is here
no easy return to old tonality—I feel there can be no short cuts
to a new musical simplicity by these means, but than tonality might
be extended to furnish new methods of cohesion."[11] Thus the
half-way stage between octave B is not F♯ as in the traditional
tonal thinking, instead the tritone E♯ is introduced as an exact
"geographical" half-way between the two poles. This is a method
that Bartók experimented with in a superlative way in his *Music
for Strings, Percussion, and Celesta* in 1936 (in the first movement).
The traditional four movement structure of the symphony is not
altered by Davies in his three symphonies. The finale of the Symphony No. 2 echoes the passacaglia idea of Brahms's Symphony
No. 4, albeit in an episodic form. These symphonies also show
that the fundamentally romantic nature of Davies, often hiding
behind the parody and the grotesque, has gained the upper hand
in his musical thinking. Those who have followed his creative development since the 1960s are now witnessing a creative synthesis
in which, through his symphonies, the European history of music
from the Gregorian chant to the present is not so much parodied,
but rather summoned into architectural and monumental sound

edifices. That is why Davies has returned not only to the classical/
romantic symphony, but also, via his reevaluation of the symphonic form, to Bruckner, Mahler, and Sibelius. The Symphony
No. 3 (1985) is the summation of this phase. Its first movement—
Lento-allegro alla breve—opens with a slow introductory section
that starts with a drumroll and that establishes the tonal/modal
point of D. As in the Symphony No. 2 the introduction of the
characteristic diminished fifth appears. The thematic material
employed is based on plainsong. The second movement—*ScherzoI-
Allegro*—and the third movement—*Scherzo II—allegro vivace*—are
linked into a structural whole within the outer movements and
are further related by the use of similar materials. The composer
has explained his musical intentions by using an analogy:

> It is as if one experiences some musical equivalent of a nave, where
> the eye progresses towards the altar from a fixed central point with
> all the proportions revealed and the side-chapels partly exposed,
> throughout the second movement,—and with a disturbed experience
> of the same seen from a side arcade, in the third. All the dimensions,
> in their second movement order lines become slightly skew-whiff, and
> quicker, in the third—i.e. the vantage point is no longer static. I have
> interrupted the third movement by letting in "windows" which, to-
> wards its conclusion, and taking the place of a "trio," open out to
> give brief glimpses towards the finale—a device I have shamelessly
> borrowed from the "Burlesque" of Mahler's Ninth Symphony, which
> also concludes with a slow movement.[12]

In the finale—*Lento*—the music expands and reaches its grandiose climax and resolution. As a whole, this work is a modern
symphonic masterpiece in which Davies, without compromising
his style or becoming an imitator, succeeds in resurrecting the
Mahlerian concept of the romantic symphony and fuses it with
the contemporary avant-garde in a convincing manner.

At present he is not only the leading figure of English contemporary music, but also one of the most charismatic and original
musical thinkers of today. His music covers the whole range of
expression from works for children to the opera and the symphony. In each genre he has left the impact of his musical genius,
characterized by an intellectual and emotional intensity, as well as
mystic vision. He was, and still is, as *The No. 11 Bus* (1984)—in
which he makes fun of the apocalypse—illustrates, an *enfant terri-*

ble of the avant-garde. Yet his romantic temperament, combined with his deeply rooted understanding of the past on which his music largely relies and to which it makes constant reference, gives a conservative twist to his avant-garde standing. Is this perhaps the ultimate parody: the artist as jester, the conservative *enfant terrible?* It seems that the "Englishness of English music" is conservatism even when it finds itself in the avant-garde.

Epilogue

That there is an abundance of British musical talent is manifested in the fact that another book could be written on those twentieth-century British composers who have been excluded from this short history. Composers such as Edmund Rubbra, Alan Rawsthorne, Alan Bush, Herbert Howells, Havergal Brian, Malcolm Arnold, and Richard Rodney Bennett immediately come to mind; their works, too, represent aspects of British music-making that are well worth studying. But the aim has not been to give an encyclopedia entry on all British composers of this century. For this, the reader is advised to turn to the splendid *New Grove Dictionary of Music and Musicians,* and, for more detailed discussion of individual composers, to the books listed in the bibliography. The aim of this book has been to guide the reader towards the works of those composers who, in a marked way, represent genres and lines of development in the twentieth-century British musical scene. The temptation of giving brief mentions of the kind "also significant is the sensuous Wilfrid Mellers," or "the distinguished, but slow-working Hugh Wood," etc., has been carefully avoided.

A reader who is able to argue that composer X could have been included in chapter Y will have proved his understanding of it.

Notes

Chapter 1. Romanticism and Postromanticism: Edward Elgar, Frederick Delius, Arnold Bax, John Ireland

1. Frederick Delius, "At the Cross Roads," *The Sackbut,* September 1920, 205.
2. Frederick Delius to Philip Heseltine, 23 June 1912, Add. MS 52547-9, British Library; also quoted in Lionel Carley and Robert Threlfall, *Delius: A Life in Pictures* (Oxford: Oxford University Press, 1977), 60.

Chapter 3. The Past into the Present: Folk-Music, the English Carol, the Choral Tradition, the Beginning of Musical Scholarship, Impressionism

1. Quoted in *An Encyclopedia of Quotations about Music,* Nat Shapiro, comp. and ed. (London: David and Charles, 1978), 128.
2. Peter Pirie, *The English Musical Renaissance: Twentieth-Century British Composers and Their Works* (London: Gollancz, 1979, 20.
3. Interview with Zoltán Kodály, reported by the Hungarian News Service, December 1962.
4. Frank Howes, *The English Musical Renaissance* (London: Secker and Warburg, 1966), 80.

Chapter 4. Modernists in the Making: Frank Bridge, Arthur Bliss, William Walton, Constant Lambert

1. Neville Cardus, "Walton's First Symphony," *Manchester Guardian* 7 November 1935.

Chapter 5. Major Minor Masters: Ivor Gurney, Peter Warlock, E.J. Moeran, Gerald Finzi

1. James Reeves, *Georgian Poetry* (Harmondsworth: Penguin Books, 1962), xvii.

2. Stephen Banfield, *Sensibility and English Song* (Cambridge: Cambridge University Press, 1985): 1:272.

3. Ibid., 1:227.

Chapter 6. A Genius with a Common Touch: Benjamin Britten

1. Scott Goddard, *British Music of Our Time* (Harmondsworth: Penguin Books, 1946), 203.

2. Benjamin Britten, *Peter Grimes*, Sadlers' Wells Opera Books, no. 3 (London: Sadlers' Wells Opera, 1946), 8.

3. Benjamin Britten, sleeve notes to his *Curlew River* (Decca Records, 1BB101–3, 1971).

Chapter 7. In Search of New Sounds: The Continental Influence: Roberto Gerhard, Egon Wellescz, Mátyás Sieber, Elizabeth Luytens, Humphrey Searle, Thea Musgrave

1. Francis Routh, *Contemporary British Music* (London: Macdonald, 1972), 30.

2. Humphrey Searle and Robert Layton, *Britain, Scandinavia and the Netherlands*, vol. 3 of *Twentieth-Century Composers* (London: Weidenfeld and Nicolson, 1972), 109.

Chapter 8. A Child of Our Time: Michael Tippett

1. Michael Tippett, sleeve notes to his *The Vision of Saint Augustine* (RCA, RL89498, 1972).

2. Simone Weil, *Gravity and Grace* (London: Routledge, 1952), 135.

Chapter 9. The Younger Generation: Alexander Goehr, Harrison Birtwhistle, Cornelius Cardew, Roger Smalley, John Taverner

1. Roger Sessions, *The Musical Experience of Composer, Performer, Listener* (Princeton, N.J.: Princeton University Press, 1950), 170.

2. Routh, *Contemporary British Music*, 314.

Chapter 10. The Conservative *enfant terrible:* Peter Maxwell Davies

1. Quoted in Parul Griffiths, *Peter Maxwell Davies* (London: Robson Books, 1982), 137.

2. Ibid., 138.

3. Ibid., 139.
4. Ibid., 141.
5. Ibid., 145–46.
6. Ibid., 149.
7. Ibid., 150.
8. Ibid., 154.
9. Ibid., 162.
10. Ibid., 171–72.
11. Ibid., 173.
12. Peter Maxwell Davies, sleeve notes to his *Symphony No. 3* (BBC Enterprises REGL 560, 1985).

Glossary

Aleatory or **Aleatoric** derives from the Latin *alea,* meaning dice, and hence the chance inherent in throwing a dice. It is a synonym for chance and indeterminacy and refers to a composition that cannot be determined before its performance, or to a work that is created by using chance, as for example, a music manuscript paper that is dotted haphazardly and that thus produces a score on which the pitches are not predetermined.

Atonal music negates the gravitational forces of tonal music by avoiding and undermining the tendency to write in a "key" or key center. References that could support a key, for example, triads, dominant-tonic cadential relationships, scales, the use of octaves, and so on, are also avoided. This inevitably results in dissonant and chromatic sound effects that create tension and unsettledness; the traditional concept of consonance and dissonance is no longer applied.

Chance music. *See* Aleatory.

Chromatic, a word meaning color (from Greek, *chromos*), in music refers to the use of notes not belonging to the diatonic scale (for example, in C major, F♯ is a chromatic note as it does not belong to the scale of C major). Within an octave as from C to c an octave higher, there are twelve chromatic semitones.

Classical symphone structure is a term in general use that refers to the outline of a classical or romantic symphony. These were usually written in four contrasting movements: fast, slow, minuet-trio-minuet (or scherzo-trio-scherzo), fast (finale). The terms also implies that at least one of the movements (usually the first) is written in sonata form.

Diatonic is the opposite of chromatic and signifies those notes of the scale that make up the characteristic major or minor scales (for example C D E F G A B C = C major).

Electronic music is a style that uses sounds produced not on traditionally made instruments played by performers, but by electronic means, such as tape or more sophisticated machines, like the synthesizer.

Expressionism is a borrowed term from art that refers to a group of German and Scandinavian painters: Nolde, Kirchner, Kokoschka, Kandinsky, and Munch. They aimed at expressing the subconscious and cultivated a style that was often nightmarish and emotional. In music, expressionism is largely found in the works of Schoenberg, Berg, and Webern. It is a style that particularly suits atonal and serial compositional methods.

Impressionism is, like expressionism, a term borrowed from art. It denotes a style that aims at hinting and evocation rather than at definite statements and so largely relies on atmosphere and therefore on color and light. In music, similar effects were achieved by Debussy, who is often equated with the French painters of the period: Monet, Renoir, and others.

Modal refers to a scale system that preceded the major-minor tonal system and that was superseded by it during the seventeenth century. Modal music is based on church modes—a medieval system of scales, such as the Dorian, Phrygian, and Lydian, each of which represents a characteristic scale structure of intervals (for example, D E F G A B C D = the Dorian mode).

Modern is a general reference to the twentieth century. *Modernism* however, is more specific in that it emphasises developments, especially in the arts, between 1890 and 1930. The term postmodernism, now also in common parlance, refers to the period after 1930.

Musique concrète ("concrete music") is music that draws on recorded sounds of all kinds, man-made or natural, for its compositional material. Originally these were not electronically distorted, but the distinction between concrete and electronic music has become increasingly blurred.

Music theater is a new kind of entertainment characterized by a blending of music, drama, speech, dance, economical staging, and lighting effects, usually in a rather expressionistic manner.

Nationalism in music achieved its full force in the nineteenth century. Its aim was to emphasize the characteristics of a nation by drawing on folk songs and dances, as well as on subjects based on native life and history.

Neoclassicism emerged as a reaction against the subjective emotionalism of the late-nineteenth-century romantic style. Some composers of the 1920s turned back to the ideas of such earlier masters as Bach, Mozart, and Vivaldi. As a result, the mammoth romantic orchestra was dropped in favor of smaller ensembles, and the old musical forms and textures, such as concerto grosso, divertimento, fugue, and passacaglia, came back into vogue, but now in a modern harmonic and rhythmic context.

Polytonality is the simultaneous sounding of more than two keys. The simultaneous sound of of two keys is called *bitonality*.

Program music is inspired by an extramusical idea (that is, legend, history, picture, or literature) that the composer sets out to describe by purely musical means.

Second Viennese School is a general reference to a group of composers who worked in Vienna in the first quarter of this century, notably Schoenberg, Berg, and Webern. (The first Viennese School was Haydn, Mozart, and Beethoven.) The styles of the members of the Second Viennese School cover late romanticism, expressionism, atonality and, finally, their adoption of the serial technique.

Serial music is one of the most radical twentieth-century developments in music. Its starting point is atonality, but whereas atonality is not an organized system, serialism is. The randomness of extreme chromaticism and atonality was formalized by Schoenberg into a series of twelve semitones that can then be organised by the composer in such a way that it serves him with a chromatic melody and harmony for the whole of the composition. A series thus constructed can be played backwards, in inversion, and so on. Schoenberg's Suite, op. 25, is based on the following series or twelve-tone row:

$$\text{E F G D}^\flat \text{ G}^\flat \text{ E}^\flat \text{ A}^\flat \text{ D B C A B}^\flat$$

This system was developed further by introducing the serialization of duration and rhythm among other things.

Sonata form refers to the structure of a movement that usually appears in the first movement of a sonata, symphony, string quartet, etc. The characteristic pattern of this form falls into three sections called *exposition, development,* and *recapitulation.* In the exposition the thematic material is "exposed" or presented both melodically and tonally, for example, *First Subject* in the tonic key (for example, C major), *Second Subject* in the dominant key (G major). The development section further evolves the thematic material that was stated in the exposition. In the recapitulation, the thematic material returns but with a major modification—both the first subject and the second subject are now tonally reconciled and are played in the tonic key.

Sprechstimme ("speaking voice") is a technique that uses a voice midway between speaking and singing. Pitches are approximated.

Tonality denotes the system in which European music was written from about the seventeenth century to the beginning of the twentieth century and beyond. The term is synonymous with key, that is, with the gravitational forces inherent in a chosen note, the tonic or tonic key. Tonal music is the opposite of atonal music.

Twelve-note music. *See* Serial music.

Dates of Composers Mentioned in the Text

Arnold: b. 1921
Auric: 1899–1983
Bach, J. S.: 1685–1750
Bartók: 1881–1945
Bax: 1883–1953
Beethoven: 1770–1827
Bennett: b. 1936
Berg: 1885–1935
Berio: b. 1925
Berkeley: b. 1903
Berlioz: 1803–69
Birtwistle: b. 1934
Bliss: 1891–1975
Blitheman: ?–1601
Boulez: b. 1925
Boyce: 1710–79
Brahms: 1833–97
Brian: 1876–1972
Bridge: 1879–1941
Britten: 1913–76
Bruch: 1838–1920
Bruckner: 1824–96
Bull: ca. 1562–1628
Butterworth: 1885–1916
Byrd: 1543–1623
Cage: b. 1912
Cardew: 1936–81
Corelli: 1653–1713
Couperin: 1668–1733
Dallapiccola: 1904–75
Debussy: 1862–1918
Delius: 1862–1934
Dieren: 1887–1936
Dunstable: ca. 1385–1453
Elgar: 1857–1934
Falla: 1876–1946
Fauré: 1845–1924
Field: 1782–1837

Finzi: 1901–56
Fricker: 1920–90
Gal: 1890–1987
Gay: 1685–1732
Gerhard: 1896–1970
Gershwin: 1898–1937
Gibbons: 1583–1625
Gluck: 1714–87
Goehr: b. 1932
Grainger: 1882–1961
Granados: 1867–1916
Grieg: 1843–1907
Gurney: 1890–1937
Hába: 1893–1973
Handel: 1685–1759
Haydn: 1732–1809
Hindemith: 1895–1963
Holst: 1874–1934
Howells: 1892–1983
Ireland: 1879–1962
Ives: 1874–1954
Janáček: 1854–1928
Josquin: ca. 1460–1521
Kodály: 1882–1967
Lambert: 1905–51
Leibowitz: 1913–72
Liszt: 1811–86
Lutyens: 1906–83
Machaut: ca. 1300–77
Mahler: 1860–1911
Maxwell Davies: b. 1934
Mendelssohn: 1809–47
Messiaen: b. 1908
Milhaud: 1892–1974
Milner: b. 1925
Moeran: 1894–1950
Monteverdi: 1567–1643
Morley: 1557–1602

Mozart: 1756–91
Musgrave: b. 1928
Mussorgsky: 1839–81
Ockeghem: ca. 1430–95
Parry: 1848–1918
Pedrell: 1841–1922
Perotin: ca. 1168–ca. 1240
Poulenc: 1899–1963
Prokofiev: 1891–1953
Puccini: 1858–1924
Purcell: 1659–95
Rachmaninov: 1873–1943
Rameau: 1683–1764
Ravel: 1875–1937
Rawsthorne: 1905–71
Rossini: 1792–1868
Rubbra: 1901–86
Satie: 1866–1925
Schmitt: 1870–1958
Schoenberg: 1874–1951
Schubert: 1797–1828
Schumann: 1810–56
Scriabin: 1872–1915
Searle: 1915–82
Seiber: 1905–60
Sessions: 1896–1985

Sharp: 1859–1924
Shostakovich: 1906–75
Sibelius: 1865–1957
Smalley: b. 1943
Smyth: 1858–1944
Souster: b. 1943
Stanford: 1852–1924
Stockhausen: b. 1928
Strauss, R.: 1864–1949
Stravinsky: 1882–1971
Tallis: ca. 1505–85
Tavener: b. 1944
Taverner: ca. 1495–1545
Tchaikovsky: 1840–93
Tippett: b. 1905
Varèse: 1883–1965
Vaughan Williams: 1872–1958
Vivaldi: 1678–1741
Wagner: 1813–83
Walton: 1902–83
Warlock: 1894–1930
Webern: 1883–1945
Weill: 1900–50
Wellesz: 1885–1974
Wood: b. 1932
Zemlinsky: 1872–1942

Bibliography

General

Banfield, Stephen. *Sensibility and English Song: Critical Studies of the Early Twentieth Century.* Cambridge: Cambridge University Press, 1985.

Griffiths, Paul. *New Sounds New Personalities: British Composers of the 1980's in Conversation with Paul Griffiths.* London: Faber and Faber, 1985.

Griffiths, Paul. *The Thames and Hudson Encyclopedia of Twentieth-Century Music.* London: Thames and Hudson, 1986.

Herman, Alec, and Wilfrid Mellers. *Man and His Music.* London: Barrie and Rockliff, 1962.

Howes, Frank. *The English Musical Renaisance.* London: Secker and Warburg, 1966.

Mackerness, E. D. *A Social History of English Music.* London: Routledge and Kegan Paul, 1964.

Pirie, Peter J. *The English Musical Renaissance: Twentieth-Century British Composers and Their Works.* London: Gollancz, 1979.

Routh, Francis. *Contemporary British Music.* London: Macdonald, 1972.

Sadie, Stanley, ed. *New Grove Dictionary of Music and Musicians.* London: Macmillan, 1980.

Schafer, Murray. *British Composers in Interview.* London: Faber and Faber, 1963.

Scholes, Percy. *The Mirror of Music, 1844–1944: A Century of Musical Life in Britain as Reflected in the Pages of the Musical Times.* 2 vols. London and Oxford: Novello and Oxford University Press, 1947.

Searle, Humphrey, and Robert Layton. *Twenteith-century Composers.* Vol. 3, *Britain, Scandinavia and the Netherlands.* London: Weidenfeld and Nicolson, 1972.

Trend, Michael. *The Music-Makers: The English Musical Renaissance from Elgar to Britten.* London: Weidenfeld and Nicolson, 1985.

Composers and Topics
in order of appearance in the text

Kennedy, Michael. *Portrait of Elgar.* Oxford: Oxford University Press, 1982.

Parrott, Ian. *Elgar.* Master Musician Series. London: Dent, 1971.

Hurd, Michael. *Elgar.* London: Faber and Faber, 1969.

Fenby, Eric. *Delius as I Knew Him.* London: Faber and Faber, 1981.

Hutchings, Arthur. *Delius, a Critical Biography.* London: Macmillan, 1948.

Jefferson, Allan. *Delius.* Master Musician Series. London: Dent, 1972.

Carley, Lionel, and Robert Threlfall. *Delius: A Life in Pictures.* Oxford: Oxford University Press, 1977.

Bax, Arnold. *Farewell My Youth.* London: Longman Green, 1943.

Foreman, Lewis. *Bax: A Composer and His times.* London: Scolar Press, 1983.

Scott-Sutherland, Colin. *Arnold Bax.* London: Dent, 1973.

Scott-Sutherland, Colin. *John Ireland.* London: Triad Press, 1980.

Searl, Muriel V. *John Ireland: The Man and His Music.* London: Midas Books, 1979.

Sharp, Cecil. *English Folk-songs, Some Conclusions.* London: Heinemann, Mercury Books, 1965.

Dickinson, A. B. F. *Vaughan Williams.* London: Faber and Faber, 1963.

Kennedy, Michael. *The Works of Ralph Vaughan Williams.* Oxford: Oxford University Press, 1964.

Hurd, Michael. *Vaughan Williams.* London: Faber and Faber, 1970.

Vaughan Williams, Ursula. *R. V. W.: A Biography of Ralph Vaughan Williams.* Oxford: Oxford University Press, 1964.

Holst, Imogen. *Holst.* London: Faber and Faber, 1981.

Hoolst, Imogen. *The Music of Gustav Holst.* Oxford: Oxford University Press, 1968.

Bird, John. *Percy Grainger.* London: Faber and Faber, 1982.

Routley, Erik. *The English Carol.* London: Herbert Jenkins, 1958.

Pirie, Peter J. *Frank Bridge.* London: Triad Press, 1971.

Bliss, Arthur. *As I Remember.* London: Faber and Faber, 1970.

Palmer, Christopher. *Bliss.* London: Novello, 1976.

Howes, Frank. *The Music of William Walton.* Oxford: Oxford University Press, 1974.

Shead, Richard. *Constant Lambert.* London: Simon, 1973.

Lambert, Constant. *Music Ho! A Study of Music in Decline.* London: Faber and Faber, 1966.

Hurd, Michael. *The Ordeal of Ivor Gurney.* Oxford: Oxford University Press, 1978.

Copley, I. A. *The Music of Peter Warlock: A Critical Survey.* London: Denis Dobson, 1979.

Gray, Cecil. *Peter Warlock.* London: Cape, 1934.

Wild, Stephen. *E. J. Moeran.* London: Triad Press, 1973.

Goddard, Scott. "Benjamin Britten." In *British Music of Our Time, edited by A. L. Bacharach, 203–12.* London: Pelican Books, 1946.

Holst, Imogen. *Britten.* London: Faber and Faber, 1980.

Headington, Christopher. *Britten.* London: Eyre Methuen, 1981.

Evans, Peter. *The Music of Benjamin Britten.* London: Dent, 1979.

Herbert, David. *The Operas of Benjamin Britten.* London: Hamish Hamilton, 1979.

Mitchell, Donald, and John Evans. *Benjamin Britten: 1913–76: Pictures from a Life.* London: Faber and Faber, 1978.

Palmer, Christopher. *The Britten Companion.* London: Faber and Faber, 1984.

White, Walter Eric. *Benjamin Britten: His Life and Operas.* London: Faber and Faber, 1983.

Kennedy, Michael. *Britten.* Master Musician Series. London: Dent, 1981.

Whittall, Arnold. *The Music of Britten and Tippett: Studies in Themes and Techniques.* Cambridge: Cambridge University Press, 1982.

Lutyens, Elizabeth. *A Goldfish Bowl.* London: Cassell, 1972.

Kemp, Ian. *Michael Tippett, A Symposium on His Sixtieth Birthday.* London: Faber and Faber, 1965.

White, Eric Walter. *Tippett and His Operas.* London: Barrie and Jenkins. 1979.

Matthews, David. *Michael Tippett: An Introductory Study.* London: Faber and Faber, 1980.

Hurd, Michael. *Tippett.* London: Novello, 1978.

Bowen, Meirion. *Michael Tippett.* London: Robson Books, 1982.

Tippett, Michael. *Moving into Aquarius.* London: Paladin Books, 1974.

Bowen, Meirion, ed. *Music of the Angels: Essays and Sketchbooks of Michael Tippett.* London: Eulenberg Books, 1980.

Hall, Michael. *Harrison Birtwistle.* The Contemporary Composer Series. London: Robson Books, 1984.

Pruslin, Stephen, ed. *Peter Maxwell Davies: Studies from Two Decades.* London: Boosey and Hawke, 1979.

Griffiths, Paul. *Peter Maxwell Davies.* London: Robson Books, 1982.

Index

T